NIGHT SCHOOL

VOLUME II

CYPRIAN'S OFFICES OF SPIRITS

Night School: Volume II
Cyprian's Offices of Spirits
Copyright © 2024 Jake Stratton-Kent
Interior images by Dis Albion and by Erzebet Barthold (sublunar sphere, p. 4).
French translations © Mary Guyver, with many thanks.

ISBN 978-1-914166-32-7 (Hardcover)
ISBN 978-1-914166-33-4 (Paperback)

A catalogue for this title is available from the British Library.
10 9 8 7 6 5 4 3 2 1

First published in 2024
Hadean Press
West Yorkshire
England

www.hadeanpress.com

NIGHT SCHOOL

VOLUME II

CYPRIAN'S OFFICES OF SPIRITS

Or

THE TERRESTRIAL INTELLIGENCER

Including

THE MAGIC OF THE LUNAR MANSIONS

THE TRUE NATURE OF THE ELEMENTAL KINGS AND QUEENS
AND THE ORIGINS OF THEIR RECEIVED NAMES

JAKE STRATTON-KENT

ACKNOWLEDGEMENTS

Thanks, in no particular order, to Alexandra Nagel for her insights into Mather's elemental marriage, to Simone Baldacci for his ear on all matters Hephaestean, to Felix Castro Vicente for introducing me to Cyprian's *Heptameron*, and Geoffrey Samuel – my 'correspondent from abroad' – for rekindling my interest therein. Honour too to the august shades of Nathaniel Moulth and Sir Walter Scott. To my personal hero Cyrano de Bergerac for being quotable in this book. To the great Paracelsus and his amanuensis and interlocutor, the Comte de Gabalis. My thanks as ever to my editor, the mighty Erzebet Barthold, and to the long-suffering Chris Carr for coping with more tables and other figures than any of my previous works. To Pepe Panda Dpw and Dreika Mücke Hacková for their hospitality and friendship on my peregrinations. To all of my friends, readers and patrons for their support and patience with my non-existent schedules. Finally, to my friend Robin Black for encouraging the writing of the Night School series.

ABBREVIATIONS USED

Attrib. Attributed

BM. *The Magus or Celestial Intelligencer*. Francis Barrett. Lackington, Allen, and Co. 1801.

Letters. *Letters on Witchcraft and Demonology*. Sir Walter Scott. London 1830.

LMEC. *Lunar Mansions and Early Calendars*. Stefan Weinstock. The Journal of Hellenic Studies Vol. 69. 1949.

PGM, PDM. *The Greek Magical Papyri in Translation, including the Demotic spells*. Hans Dieter Betz (Editor). University of Chicago Press. 1986, 1992.

PMDS. *Petit Manuel du Devin et du Sorcier*. Nathaniel Moulth. Passard, Libraire-Editeur. Paris. 1854.

TBOP. *Three Books of Occult Philosophy*. Cornelius Agrippa. Translated by James Freake. London: 1651.

TCM. *The Testament of Cyprian the Mage*. Jake Stratton-Kent. Scarlet Imprint. 2016.

But *Magic*, according to the Greeks, is a thing of a very powerful nature. *For they say that this forms the last part of the sacerdotal science.* Magic, indeed, investigates the nature, power, and quality of everything sublunary; viz. of the elements and their parts, of animals, all-various plants and their fruits, of stones and herbs: and in short, it explores the essence and power of every thing. From hence, therefore, it produces its effects.

Michael Psellus, *On Daemons according to the Dogmas of the Greeks*, p. 293.

Contents

On Terrestrial Intelligence:

A Foreword

We are extraordinarily fortunate to have this *Terrestrial Intelligencer* from the late Jake Stratton-Kent, which – having been written as (in Jake's own words) a 'twenty-first-century conjure primer' – ably addresses multiple angles of magical exploration and practice.

The wonderfully old-school running title frontispiece of this collection of terrestrial intelligence lets the reader know immediately three core themes of this work: Cyprianic spirit-work; the magics and mysteries of the Lunar Mansions; and ongoing investigation of – not to mention appreciation for – the Kings and Queens of the Elementals. To this we can additionally foreground themes of practical sublunary cosmology (especially the importance of the Underworld in such worldviews and schema of magical practice), talisman-craft, ritual calendrics, and the significance of local folkloric spirits in traditional grimoiric sorcery, spellcraft, and spiritwork.

The first contribution of this follow-up volume in the *Night School* series fills in an important lacuna in the study and practice of the Cyprianic magic of the English grimoire traditions. Specifically, it addresses the apparent lack of clarity about how exactly one might perform a 'Mass of Saint Cyprian', a ritual action demanded by the consecrations and empowerments of Cyprianic manuals of spirit conjuration such as the sixteenth-century *De Nigromancia*. Approaching ritual liturgy as a sorcerer, Jake's 'Collect of Saint Cyprian' offers liturgists of all shades of Christian and pagan an example of one such means by which a Mass might be additionally dedicated to and empowered by this infamous sorcerer saint Cyprian of Antioch.

In the 'Theologicon', we have some of the clearest practical guidance committed to print of Jake's conceptions of a seven-fold as well as four-fold sublunary cosmology; once more championing the importance of the Underworld in our occult philosophising, not to mention in our sorcerous actions and practices. We are presented with historical contexts and comparisons to better understand the utility of this sevenfold schema, as well as recommendations about highly practical grimoiric implementations and explorations of this more nuanced and enspirited model of the sublunary realms. Practitioners whose *goetia* draws from the *Grimoire of Pope Honorius* – especially its assignments of unclean spirits to the days of the week – and of course those who work with Jake's beloved *Grimorium Verum* will certainly appreciate the ways JSK weaves rich and expansive cosmology into and out of spirit catalogues, protocols, and offices here.

This practical terrestrial intelligencing continues with a brace of concise writings on conceptions of the sublunary sphere(s) in antiquity and reflections on just how much more use we sorcerers, witches, and modern cunning-folk can get out of a Three Worlds model. Following this weaponised cosmology we come rather naturally to some 'Astrological Considerations' – a title which should itself be appreciated for its stellar wordplay – which range from observations of the shifting fortunes of astrological magic in contemporary occulture to a gloriously pointed "introductory rant" on what to do about 'rite timing', experimentation, and unlearning unhelpful cultural conceptions for working astrologically.

A concise and once-more eminently practical guide to beginning to work with the Lunar Mansions proceeds from all of this cosmologising, and pinpoints where the potencies of all manner of starry wisdoms, weapons, and medicines can be filtered through the ever-turning motions of that glorious Queen and Key of the Stars, our own dear Luminary of the Night, the Moon. Never one to shirk from contention or fruitful disagreement, JSK points out a variety of difficulties in the study and practice of lunar magics of these sorts, and frequently chimes in with his own pragmatic advice and perspectives on such variances of opinion.

Another set of Jake's great passions is ably summarised in the title of the next section – 'Hecate and the Dactyls in the Papyri' – a chapter sure to have PGM magicians reaching for their copies of Betz and goetic magicians thumbing back through *Geosophia*. This focused study considers – amongst other things – the formulae, sounds, and symbols of Hecate in ancient Greco-Egyptian magic not only as historical exemplars but vivid and potent means to explore both initiation and sorcerous operations in Underworldly contexts. Weaving the twenty-eight forms of lunary titan-goddesses into and out of Mansion-work, Jake leaves the reader with a great sense of the utility, flexibility, and potency of such forms of magical work. Once more, such lunary scheming is also tabulated with grimoiric understandings, ritual calendrics, and prompts to further exploration of the powers and purviews of the spirits of the *True Grimoire*.

The following chapter, 'The Lunar Mansions and the Blue Grimoires', combines an overview of the Albertine magics of the so-called "blue grimoires" with analysis and practical consideration of a little-known grimoire, the *Petit Manuel du Devin et du Sorcier* by Nathaniel Moulth. Developing themes explored in his *Testament of Cyprian the Mage*, this chapter examines approaches to planetary talismans and images, Greco-Egyptian deities, and elemental spirits, offering close reading of the offices and asterisms of the chiefs of spirits in Moulth's *Little Manual* to explore historical contexts for approaching the Elemental Kings and Queens – Niksa, Paralda, Ghob, and Djin – from explicitly goetic contexts and ritual operations. This marks an especially significant contribution to grimoiric study and practice, since a good case is made for the goetic (not to mention sabbatic) contexts of the Elemental Kings and Queens far preceding the rather confused later attributions of element and direction to these senior spirits by Eliphas Levi.

Developing this study of Moulth's *Petit Manuel*, 'Baalberith and the Sabbat' further explicates research and understanding of the rather enigmatic spirit Leonard from the Cyprianic *Magical Elements* and further builds on earlier work both in Jake's *Testament of Cyprian* and *Pandemonium*. Notes on Lucifuge Rofocale and the Syrach/Syrachi/Scirlin complex should prove especially useful for nigromantic grimoirists. This section also generously affords us extended excerpts from Moulth's *Little Manual* exploring Sabbatic frameworks and contexts of this goetia, before the following chapter launches into detailed analysis and cross-comparison of the treatment of Paralda, Queen of the Sylphs, and the aerial domains of the Sylphide peoples, ably contextualising wider and deeper work with the Elemental Kingdoms from Paracelsian and Albertine approaches.

Synthesizing all of this context into the proceeding chapter on 'Practical implications', Jake explores the demonological angles of the Lunar Mansions in light of Albertine considerations of astrological talismans. Particular attention is paid to animal forms and sigils for such talismanic engagements. Finally, a dedicated section further assesses the magical materials useful for effective work with the Behenian Stars. Here we find further helpful tabulations of stone, star, and herb, along with plant, sigil, and answering *Verum* spirit.

A concluding chapter, aptly titled simply 'Practice', takes the reader through beginning to work with this material in their own practical experiments of spirit-work and talisman-craft, offering valuable insights and guidance on integrating traditional forms, iconography, *materia*, and concordantly stirred occult virtues. A range of options about how to engage with these favoured loci of the spirits are presented, along with some insightful glimpses into Jake's own work with that potent spirit of the *GV*, Frimost.

Helpful tables further cross-referencing Moulth's spirit catalogue with the Cyprianic *Heptameron* follow, as well as analysis of their stated ranks and interrelationships. Jake's reordering and restoration of somewhat confused star and spirit correspondences are explicated and tabulated to afford greater integration with Lunar Mansion schema. Far from simply churning out armchaired equivalencies, these considerations are explicitly grounded as providing deeper understanding of all these elemental and folkloric spirits as not only sublunary but contributing to the rich thronging spirit ecologies of the Mansions themselves.

Attentions are also paid to the elemental (pseudo)angelology advanced by Moulth in light of Paracelsian iconoclasm and the rehabilitation of the spirits of traditional grimoiric goetia as elementals. Here JSK once more reminds karcists of a more nigromantic persuasion not to be put off work with spirits merely labeled angelic; for as these case studies demonstrate 'plainly "angels" as a category is elastic enough to comprehend both hobgoblins and the lower pagan deities.' Tables of the Elemental Genii and their 'cohorts' further operationalise the material in Moulth's manual, as excerpts from the writings of Walter Scott and Robert Fludd, as well as Agrippa, Paracelsus, and Albertus Magnus are offered for further eludidation of both historical understanding and sorcerous practicalities. The author also generously offers an alternative schema for integrating Mansion cusps, Verum spirits, and Agrippan Mansion angels.

Having set out these tables of spirit correspondence, Jake goes onto demonstrate the robust utility of such schemas. Refining the spirit descriptions from his *Testament* of the Cyprianic *Heptameron*, we are treated to further analysis of the identity and role of the Sibyls, another topic dear to Jake's heart. Furnished with alternative and more illuminating spellings of spirit names from these Moulthian materials, we are furthermore able to appreciate how this catalogue draws on deeply rooted European folklore of dwarves as well as Scottish *sith* and Irish *sidhe* in its spiritwork. Such analysis is not merely idle sightseeing through the grimoiric corpus; rather, it forms a further bolstering proof to Jake's considered position in commending and defending the conjuration of folkloric spirits as absolutely within the traditional purview of an operative grimoirist.

The final section of the *Terrestrial Intelligencer* proper offers us cross-examination of the Fixed Star positions in the Heavens of Summer and of Winter with features of the Lunar Mansions, including further cataloguing of starry and sublunary *materia magica* and their magical uses and applications. Finally, a grand twenty-eight-piece table of sample Fixed Star positions collated by Mansion, zodiacal degree, star name, orb, planetary influence, and other pertinent notes – along with considerations of calendrical assessment and utility of the Mansions as a stellar cartography 'against which backdrop the planets and luminaries move' – wraps all of this context and explication together in a convenient reference section.

This second volume of the *Night School* series concludes with an appendix offering extended excerpts from Agrippa's *Three Book of Occult Philosophy* on Mansion images, a translation of Mansion talismans and works from the *Picatrix*, and an afterword leaving us food for thought concerning how Jake considered and approached the living expression of archaic local cultus in his contemporary occult practice, characteristically espousing his grimoire, his spirits, and his role and worldview as a modern magician as well as – as he would sometimes quip – a "Very Late-Pagan".

Throughout this text, our author consistently shows as well as tells us how we can dispense with so many intellectual pitfalls that might dog both the beginner and expert magical practitioner alike. Time and time again, we are encouraged to abandon armchairing perfected models or worrying about pedantic academic inaccuracies, and to re-engage with our practices in and out of the messy, exciting, terrific realities of our very real world of magic, spirits, and mysteries.

At the sight of so many tables and Mansion degrees and interwoven quotes from various grimoiric texts and commentators and so on, the reader – especially the enthusiastic beginner magician for which this primer was collected – should be assured that this collection of writings stresses practicality in not only thinking about magic but in actually *doing* magic.

We are – to re-iterate – extraordinarily fortunate to have a final text from the late Jake Stratton-Kent in the form of this *Terrestrial Intelligencer*. To the point, punchy, and full of unearthed grimoiric gems, sorcerous implications, and hard-won wisdoms alike, this is a book that – like so many of Jake's works – richly gifts us with the fruits of his fierce intellect, his rabble-rousing compassion, and his decades of dedicated ritual practice and spiritwork. Published posthumously by his dear friends at Hadean Press, it seems an apt testament to Jake's tenacity and passion that even death itself could not prevent Britain's most notorious necromancer from leaving us one more haunted treasure trove to aid, counsel, and arm future generations of necromancers.

So here's to our Jakey, and to all of us who continue to benefit from his words, his works, and his memory, and to all those to come. Truly, necromancy never dies.

Dr Alexander Cummins
New England, 2024

A COLLECT OF CYPRIAN THE MAGE

(Perfume with musk, amber, storax, and frankincense.)

Remember, Lord, your servants full of praise
As they remember him who served thee in old days:
O Cyprian, vowed to Apollo in thy youth; initiate of all
Arts of the Dragon.
In thy power, speak for and defend us.
Sweet Cyprian, who as a boy attended the temple of Mithra
In thy power, speak for and defend us.
Initiate child, who bore the torches at Eleusis and lamented
for Persephone, who knew the dragon at the temple of the
Wise One.
In thy power, speak for and defend us.
Who, innocent, ascended unto the abode of the gods, knowing
their speech and holy sounds; the lore of trees and plants under
them, and all their operations with spirits.
In thy power, speak for and defend us.
For forty days you beheld the succession of seasons, the changes
of winds and the variations of the days: the mingling of the
like and the unlike. Thou saw all bands of spirits, some friends,
others enemies, the phalanx of each god and goddess. Fasting,
eating only fruits, as taught by the seven priests of the sacrifices.
In thy power, speak for and defend us.
Who as a youth learned the natural laws of generation and
corruption; of bodies earthly, aerial, and aquatic. Also, those
powers that the Lord of this World hath to adapt and turn these
from their originals.

In thy power, speak for and defend us.

In Argos you were initiated into the mysteries of Hera; learning the union of air with ether, of ether with air, and of earth with water and water with air.

In thy power, speak for and defend us.

You went also unto Elis, abode of Artemis; and learned the blending and dividing of matter and the raising of occult and ancient orations.

In thy power, speak for and defend us.

Divination you learned, as a man, from the Phrygians, the inspection of entrails, the observation of birds and the motions of animals, and all the sounds of creatures who give knowledge. The languages of woods and stones; the sounds of the dead in their graves; the noises of doors and the varied palpitations of limbs. Also, the motion of the blood and the composition of growths. Yes, all outward effects of disease upon bodies thou learned whether appearing by natural or unnatural means.

In thy power, speak for and defend us.

Thou learned the throwing of words, and numbers into words and words into numbers, and oaths implicit or explicit, and agreements in hostility.

In thy power, speak for and defend us.

Nothing on the earth, nor in the sea, nor in the air was hidden from thee, nor any kinds of spirit, nor any manner of knowledge, no changeful things, no mechanical, no artificial things.

In thy power, speak for and defend us.

Thou with complete knowledge, even to extract True Oracles from the Holy Word.

In thy power, speak for and defend us.

NOTE: in the *Nigromancia* and elsewhere, when undertaking the construction of the Circle (or of a permanent ritual chamber), it is to be consecrated by means of a mysterious 'Mass of Saint Cyprian'. Now, as I understand things, this implies an appropriate 'collect' of the Saint within an otherwise fairly conventional Mass rather than a ritual involving him at every turn. Also, as indicated in my previous works, my preferred ritual frame does include a Mass, which form is thus 'conventional' in this ritual cycle. Consequently, what is required of your liturgist author is an appropriate Collect rather than an entire Mass. In general, the time for this would be when perfuming the Circle from outside prior to new undertakings, as well as the occasion of making a permanent Circle. As will be seen, the ritual approaches him as a teacher or mentor of the Mysteries, appropriate to the theology of the frame and quite regardless of 'denominational' concerns.

THEOLOGICON

INTRODUCTORY

Throughout my magical life my reading and interests have led me again and again to places where information was scant and contemporary occult writers were unengaged. Initially this applied to the printed word: areas where academics or my own efforts had identified an area of interest were either unincluded – the general pattern – or confined to a lonely line or paragraph in modern occult works. As time went on the Internet changed the landscape, but not the pattern. Thus, on occasion, having opened up an area formerly neglected or misunderstood, I am asked where more information can be found. The expectation, naturally enough, is a website, or a book readily available online. The reality is much harder to convey, involving the habits of keeping files and following trails where non-mainstream ideas and models are concerned. Nor is it a simple matter to communicate how productive the seeds of such research are (from little acorns mighty oak trees grow), and how the accepted picture can be utterly transformed, even negated, by following such leads. Often the transformation is potentially welcome in the broader world, but accepted models do not support or gel with it sufficiently. So too, the capacity to put those models down and engage with another is harder to achieve than one might assume.

So it is that the world model assumed throughout this work, while unfamiliar, is expressible in various ways. It is minimalistic, in that it involves a simpler cosmology, however it is expressed, than does mainstream occultism. It discards entirely certain notions – and familiar diagrams – with which a great many works on 'modern magic' set out, and around which they revolve. Insofar as less assumptions in advance is a good thing, this could be seen as a sceptical experimental baseline. This is appropriate to a modern manual in a supposedly scientific age. While this is certainly a point in its favour, it is not the *only* point. Equally, these same discarded assumptions are strongly connected with Western monotheism, particularly the belief in a transcendental deity not of this world. From this perspective, the model could be seen as compatible with modern 'neopaganism' which, however, often has a habit of not examining the assumptions concerned, and simply retaining them in other forms.

Thus, in this C21st conjure primer, I propose and assume the need for clarity and versatility in 'implicit theology', besides a strong departure from those imposed or retained without discussion previously. Experience has taught me that compromising with such familiar models leads to less comprehension rather than more.

As said, the view proposed is compatible with and useful in experimenting without too many assumptions. At the same time, while generic compatibility with neopaganism is not a given, it also reflects – or accommodates – archaic belief in a useful way. Archaic lore though is communicated to us largely by myths, artefacts, and inscriptions, and understanding is ever subject to variation, dependent on grasping context. It is thus not readily invoked to clarify a working baseline in a manual such as this. Thus, I borrow instead from two models of different periods that, firstly, depart strongly from more familiar ones not useful here, while, secondly, resembling one another and communicating an outline cosmology compatible with my purposes.

In Western thought since before the Christian era and well into it, it was held that the sublunary sphere was the whole extent of changing Nature. From the Moon outwards everything was One, eternal and immutable. Physics, as such, only applied below the Moon. Not until Copernicus was this distinction challenged, until eventually Thomas Kuhn – physicist, historian, and scientific philosopher – could speak of seeing change in the 'incorruptible' heavens as the epitome of a scientific paradigm shift. Simply put, some ancient models need inverting in order to serve any purpose in modern magic. For magical purposes, the Sublunar sphere – what is Below – provides a more coherent model of what is Above than the false image of the heavens can now do for what is below. Our planetary 'superiors' can instead be subsumed into older more terrestrial guises. But I race ahead . . .

In short, this is the magical paradigm shift employed or assumed throughout the current work, both Archaic *and* harmonious with material science.

It is important to understand that the sublunar world in Late Antiquity was the so-called 'World of the Four Elements'. However, in its best, most immediately useful and most developed form, the sublunar sphere was also divided into seven, and the correspondence was extended to the planets. Dualistic qualities were often attributed to them, including moral ones: seven virtues and vices for example. This I propose to reverse, since in reality, since planetary astrology is a historical development and the cosmology involved here is far older even than history, the symbolism was – or can be considered as – having been transferred upwards rather than downwards. In other words, these sublunar spheres commemorate far earlier levels of myth and ritual, from which the qualities of the planets were extrapolated *subsequently*. This is not to deny astrology its place, whether calculatory or symbolic. The Celestial realm is one of the Three Worlds, along with our Earth and the Underworld, a subject that awaits its place.

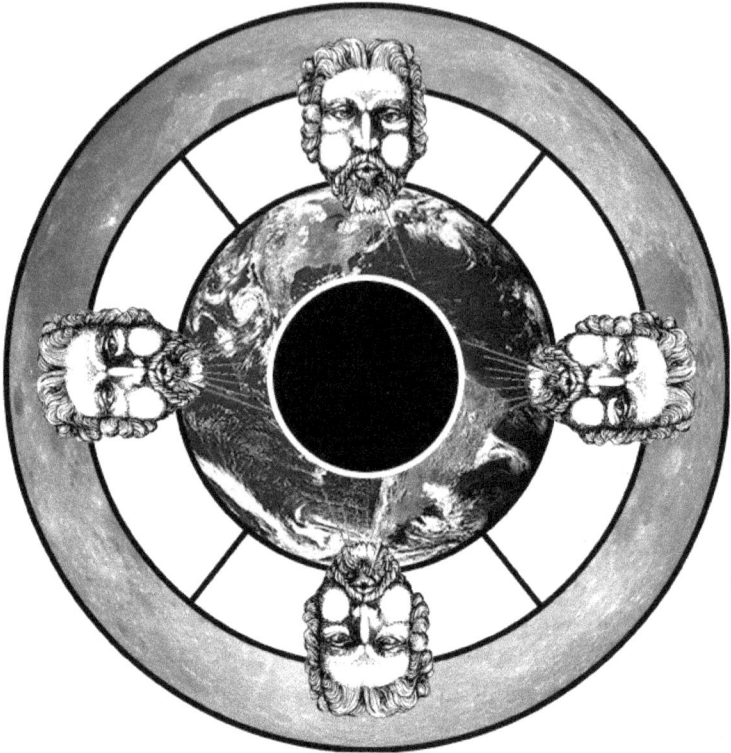

These seven are briefly definable as:

1. The Moon, uppermost, obviously enough. However, note the distinction, whereas in later schemes the Moon is depicted as inferior to the planetary and stellar worlds (besides hypothetical 'super-celestials'), in this and earlier conceptions the Moon rules the night sky, and is leader of the stars.

2-5. The four directions, attributable to winds or elements (the latter too being a historical concept are a secondary idea to directionality).

6. The Earth.

7. The Underworld.

Many occult models do not emphasise – if they even acknowledge – the importance of the Underworld as a concept, and the emergent utility of this schema begins by doing so.

We may, while bearing in mind they are secondary qualities, attribute these levels to the seven planets, of which – again – the divisions of the sublunar 'World' can be considered the prototype rather than vice versa. This attribution obviously begins with the Moon, and taking the planetary week as our model, the remainder follow in descending order: Mars, Mercury, Jupiter, Venus, Saturn, and the Sun. The careful reader will note this attribution connects the Sun with the Underworld; in astrological terms, it places him in in the IVth house, or even Midnight.

So too attributions of the elements and 'Elementals' follow. This is useful on various levels as these are fundamental to the approach to grimoire work proposed here, and thus to the Four Chiefs of spirits and their subordinates. That these were and are referred to as aerial spirits or 'spirits of the air' derives immediately from this ancient view of the region between Earth and the Moon. The distinction of 'aerial spirits', which applies to the four directions/ elements, should be carefully made. Indeed, a more significant elemental classification applies not to the directions, but to the levels. The natural order, from below, is:

Fire: corresponding to the Underworld (the Night Home of the Sun, Infernus, the Abode of the Salamanders)

Earth: corresponding to the Terrestrial region (the abode of the Gnomes)

Water: conceived firstly as Oceanus surrounding dry land, and connected to the Underworld, particularly via rivers and springs (abode of the Undines)

Air: the Aerial region above Water and Earth, the four directions of space (the abode of the sylphs and of spirits ascending to and descending from the Moon).

Above them is the Moon, ruler of the sublunar world-system, among major identities are Persephone and Hecate, both intermediary and eschatological figures, both familiar with the Underworld.

This model is rendered practical in many ways via the close accord with the spirit hierarchy of the *Grimoire of Pope Honorius*. This is – so far as is currently known – the only grimoire to use a planetary week starting deliberately and consistently on Monday. An expanded and elucidated form of its ritual patterning is as follows:

DAY OF THE WEEK	'PLANET'	SPIRIT TYPE	NAMED SPIRITS
Monday	Moon	Superiors	Lucifer, Trinitas*
Tuesday	Mars	Northern, aquatic	Frimost aka Nambroth
Wednesday	Mercury	Western, aerial	Astaroth
Thursday	Jupiter	Eastern, fiery	Sirchade
Friday	Venus	Southern, earthy	Bechet or Bechaud
Saturday	Saturn	Terrestrial	Nebiros
Sunday	Sun	Subterranean	Aciel (aka Aquiot, Aquiel, Azael)

* Trinitas refers to the ruling triad of Chiefs.

To reiterate a point made differently earlier, the elemental schema is not hard and fast. Directionality is the key quality, and – for instance – a 'fire' spirit may be found under the rule of the prince of another direction than the East, and so on. This is less problematic than might be thought, given proper understanding and empathy, rather than a mechanistic approach.

Conceptually, various 'Works of the Days' can be organised fairly readily from this table and appropriate grimoire materials. Offerings, vows, and lesser works of magic are obvious examples.

NOTES ON THE SUBLUNAR SPHERE IN ANTIQUITY

extracted from *Geosophia*, volume 1, pp. 170-74

In Plato's myth the asphodel meadow of Hades is an aerial place, in the upper atmosphere, while Tartarus remains underground. Subsequently this was extended, as in Plutarch for whom the river Styx flowed upwards from the Earth to the Moon, and the Asphodel Meadows are transferred to the space between Earth and the Moon, which luminary plays a very conspicuous part in Plutarch's eschatology:

> Every soul, whether without mind, or joined to mind, on departing from the body, is ordained to wander in the region lying between the moon and earth for a term, not equal in all cases; but the wicked and incontinent pay a penalty for their sins; whereas the virtuous, in order, as it were, to purify themselves and to recover breath, after the body, as being the source of sinful pollution, must pass a certain fixed time in the mildest region of air, which they call the Meadow of Hades. (Moralia V. *On the Cessation of Oracles.*)

Tantalisingly, Plato tells us the ritual specialists or *goetes* described themselves as 'Children of the Moon', so perhaps these lunar associations are earlier than is currently thought. In any case, in various religions of late antiquity the relocation is extended even further.

Plato's transferral of the Isles of the Blessed to indeterminate places in the heaven was soon clarified. Iamblichus — the head of the Syrian Neoplatonist school, (died 330 AD) — records a dictum attributed to the Pythagoreans locating the Isles of the Blessed in the Sun and Moon; this may represent a late, fully developed form of the process. If so, Plutarch (died 140 BCE) far precedes it by presenting an entire eschatological lunar landscape, which simultaneously illustrates the transferral of chthonic deities:

> ...there are deep places and gulf-like in the moon, whereof the largest is called Hecate's dungeon, in which the souls either suffer or inflict punishment, for the things which they have either done or endured... (Moralia. XII. On the Face in the Moon)

The schema is consciously building on Plato, the Moon is a transitional region between the lower earth and the higher planetary spheres leading to the Fixed Stars and beyond. Thus, Plutarch invests her with upper and lower portals:

> as for the two smaller depths, because the souls pass through them on the way towards heaven and towards earth back again, the one (facing the

Sun) is denominated the Elysian Plain, the other
(facing the Earth) the Passage of Persephone the
Terrestrial! (Moralia. XII. On the Face in the
Moon)

The higher worlds are occupied by the gods and their
retinues, but the Moon is the preserve of terrestrial
daimons, which is to say the dead [or which category
certainly includes the dead as a major proportion. The
very term terrestrial appears contradictory in this context,
and its use shows the pace at which ideas were evolving
while terminology struggled to keep pace. These spirits
form a very important class and are not distinct from
the souls previously mentioned. The idea of a sublunary
world between Earth and the Moon, occupied by spirits
or demons, was long enduring; it was simply forgotten that
most of them were former human beings. Reclassified as
Aerial demons, they are traceable in Agrippa and much
demonological lore, the angels being [considered] resident
higher up, in accordance with Christian Neoplatonist
ideas. The positive aspects of sub-lunar spirits have been
eradicated from many of these later redactions, along with
their identity with the dead. In Plutarch the essentially
benign role of some among the lunar terrestrial daimons is
very apparent, and he names some very interesting names:

> The daimons do not always pass their time upon
> her (the moon), but they come down hither and
> take charge of Oracles. They are present at and
> assist in the most advanced of the initiatory rites
> (Mysteries). They act as punishers and keepers of
> wrongdoers, and shine as saviours in battle and at
> sea. Whatsoever thing in these capacities they do

amiss, either out of spite, unfair partiality, or envy,
they are punished for it, for they are driven down
again to earth and coupled with human bodies.
Of the best of these genii they told him were those
who wait upon (the god) Saturn (in Elysium) now,
and the same in old times were the Idaean Dactyls
in Crete, the Curetes in Phrygia, the Trophonians
in Boeotia Lebadea, and others without number
in various parts of the world... (Moralia. XII. 'On
the Face in the Moon')

Whilst I am not suggesting that popular belief in the ancient
world faithfully adhered to the tenets of Plutarch or Plato,
there undoubtedly were popular forms of these ideas. In
fact, Plutarch was as influenced by popular traditions as he
was by Plato, and has the additional virtue of illustrating
and providing models for the subject in hand. On the
other hand under-estimating the influence of Plato and
his successors on the literate classes of the Greco-Roman
world would also be an error. What might be termed
Low Platonism was undoubtedly highly fashionable in
the later Græco-Roman world. Consequently we find his
influence in various Gnostic texts, and perfectly visible in
the Low Hermetic Magical Papyri. So far as the grimoires
are concerned, Low Neoplatonism *generally* typifies what
we might term the school of Agrippa [once the 19th
century overemphasis on the 'cabalistic' elements of his
Occult Philosophy is penetrated]. Indeed the above passage
is strikingly reminiscent of the ideas of the Comte de
Gabalis, as cited in my *True Grimoire*. His writings were
contemporary with and influential upon important
manuscript and printed grimoires.

THE THREE WORLDS

Within various ancient cosmologies, including various forms of shamanic worldview, the universe is viewed as consisting of three worlds, in sharp contrast to the Four Worlds of the Qabalah, which maps a very different view of reality. It is convenient to stratify these, as is conventionally done, in terms of upper, middle, and lower worlds. To be specific, the upper or celestial world signifies the world of the stars and planets: the day and night sky, home not only to 'astrological' gods and spirits, but those of thunder, lightning, and rain. Despite the apparent stratification and misleading comparisons thereof with 'emanation schemes', this world is best not understood as superior, but simply different. In particular it should be noted that the Sun, Moon, planets, and all but the circumpolar stars rise from the Underworld and return unto it at their setting. Thus, celestial and chthonic gods are not remotely as far apart as mere diagrams suggest.

The middle world – the Midgard of Norse mythology – not surprisingly, is the Earth, our home. Here preside gods and spirits of Nature, and also those of place (*genius loci*) and others.

The lower world is the most complex, problematic, and misunderstood, particularly if the bias derived from more familiar emanation schemes is allowed to intrude. It is the Underworld, the abode of the dead, but also of other natural spirits, associated with seeds and roots, metallic ores such as gold and iron, and also frequently with water, such as lakes, rivers and springs, and of course the Ocean. This idea can readily be found in Greek myth, where the Sea was inseparable from conceptions of the Underworld and Afterlife, and in the magic of the Greek papyri (and some later grimoires), where spring water was employed in operations of the dead. The Underworld is a complex place in these mythologies, as examined in *Geosophia*. There are 'heavenly' aspects to the

Underworld, such as the Elysian Fields or 'Isles of the Blessed'. Then too we find Hades to have similarities with Purgatory, and Tartarus with Hell, a kind of dungeon world from which there is no escape. Each of these is equally a part of the same world, rather than separate as they are in later 'transcendental' religions. This region is also frequently referred to as the home of the gods.

From this we can see that ideas of 'heaven and hell' are not appropriate to such a worldview, and that the roots of the entire cosmology are below, rather than above. This again is mirrored in ancient Greek cosmology, prior to its reworking by the philosophers. In this form, Zeus, the King of the Gods – eventually to be reworked as a deity more like Jehovah than his original self – was a son not of 'heaven', but of the Earth goddess. He shares this origin with numerous other major deities of that pantheon. Additionally, be it noted, while zodiacal and planetary classifications of the gods, plus 'Earth" goddesses and etc. are better known, the Elements are active in all three worlds, and the same classification is readily applied to working with the gods, casting a different light upon them, more apt to the approach herein.

ASTROLOGICAL CONSIDERATIONS

Never mind the interest of the subject, Magical Astrology is also a hot political issue in contemporary occultism. This is a fairly recent development; twenty-five years ago almost the only major voice on the subject was Pete Carroll denouncing the whole subject. It was moot who exactly he was denouncing, as so few occultists were even talking positively regarding rite timing, let alone employing it. Then out of the woodwork came the English Qaballistic 'school' – evidently well acquainted with Agrippa and the traditional sources, but also with Ebertin and other important moderns. They broke with tradition by investigating 'combustion' (whether Solar conjunctions or Moon in Via Combusta) among other areas recommended only for avoidance by Agrippa.

Now, of course, there is a big Internet presence for Renaissance Astrology – ably represented by Christopher Warnock. Wider occulture meanwhile seems largely oblivious to and occasionally overly dismissive of the work of intelligent moderns. There is an unevenness too in examination of Hellenistic astrology, which is the foundational level of Astrology as such. This even though Chaldean methods preceding it were extremely advanced, and built upon still older strata, from older Mesopotamian cultures and remote prehistory. Chaldean expertise and development continued throughout the Hellenistic period; indeed 'Chaldean' and 'astrologer' were more or less synonymous terms among the Romans. The unevenness is in regarding the more mythic and magical aspects of Hellenistic Astrology, often where the Egyptian influence was strongest, in favour of more 'rational' astrology ala Ptolemy. This is not to say that magic is excluded – far from it. However, comparison of Greco-Egyptian works on decan magic

with Latin ones are instructive. Latin decan images are 'allegorical',
while Egyptian images are pictures of gods and spirits, what
Albertus in his *Speculum Astronomiae* would have distinguished as
'astronomical' versus 'necromantic'.

My mentioning all this isn't to say 'more ancient is better',
but to show how three major phases of astrological history can be
usefully distinguished. Having attended a little to the when and
where, a useful preliminary examination follows, enabling critique
or assimilation for practical use now.

The problem with the modern emphasis on the collective
effect (not the school) of Renaissance Astrology is a contemporary
focus on things largely on the grounds of date of origin. A major
example is the 'Arabic Parts' extensively explored by Warnock's
predecessor and brother in spirit, Robert Zoller. In Hellenistic
Astrology there were essentially seven 'Parts', corresponding to
the Seven 'planets'. Of these the Part of Fortune and the Part
of Daimon, corresponding to Sun and Moon, were undoubtedly
the most important. The 'Arabs', who inherited Hellenistic lore
from Sabeans and Byzantines, massively extended the Parts
(and gave their name to them). My contention is that the vast
majority of these Parts are largely hypothetical, produced in
ivory towers by mathematicians employed by the Caliph of
Baghdad. Thus, the antique 'stock exchange' Parts, such as the
Part of lentils and the Part of onions, etc. etc., are accepted by
'Renaissance' astrological magicians solely because they are
'Renaissance' in date (that is, the West largely got to know of them
in that time frame). Meanwhile, the original Hellenistic Parts are
more worthy of consideration, being used by empirical Greek and
Byzantine astrologers for far longer, and without such an 'ivory
tower' background. They also have far more straightforward
magical and esoteric applications. In addition, being much less
numerous (not to mention less absurdly specialised), there is far
more scope for investigation and comparison of results (simply

add the Part of Fortune with or without the others into your astrological programme preferences and collate data).

This is not the only element of 'Renaissance' Astrology where super-Virgoan Arab astrologers who didn't have to work for a living have left their mark. The concept of 'Cazimi', where Mercury stops being combust at a particularly refined point of conjunction, is another. While calculable for an Electional chart, the likelihood of acquiring a database of reliable charts exhibiting the supposed effects are rather remote, and it has the appearance of being almost or entirely hypothetical.

So, what are we to do? Well, for a start, learn basic astrology, how to set up a chart and what the aspects and houses are about. Avoid textbooks which make this more complex than it actually is. Aleister Crowley, whose greatest fan I am far from being, did a good job of reducing the basics of chart drawing to a few paragraphs rather than a thick book! Read some decent historical accounts of the subject (Nicholas Campion and William Tester are good). Take on board what Agrippa has to say on the subject if you have the head for it, bearing in mind that he was a product of a particular period, with particular influences.

Collect charts; historical individuals and event charts are collated and published by a variety of sources, and I recommend you also keep on file those you do yourself. Avoid focus on Natal astrology alone, though by all means practice it to hone your skills and see the planets in action in that context; progressions and transits can be applied to these filed natal charts later. Nevertheless, branching out into Horary Astrology – the purely divinatory side – is a good idea, while both Electional and Mundane Astrology can be of interest magically. Elections are much used by magically inclined astrologers past and present, making comment here largely redundant. Mundane Astrology may well be of interest however, and one practice in particular is worth mentioning. A common method is to erect a 'Solar Ingress' chart for the Equinoxes and

Solstices – the precise time the Sun enters each Cardinal Sign – and draw geo-political predictions from them. That occultists of various descriptions 'celebrate' these times ritually is no coincidence, and the two practices combine readily. Having reached thus far, the world of Rite Timing is no distance at all.

When approaching astrology then, test the hypotheses promoted by the Renaissance school by all means. Do not however exclude the 'Outer Planets' or 'Trans-Saturnians' automatically from your astrological computer programme. See in fact if you can **add** features to the programme, particularly the Part of Fortune, or the other Hellenistic Parts. Be certain to learn how to erect a chart on paper, so you understand the mechanisms well enough to spot when a computer chart has errors (Sun at Midnight should not be in the Tenth House, change AM to PM!). Experiment with traditional rules, but don't consider them the be all and end all. They aren't, and knowledge of a decent number of charts will soon illustrate their shortcomings. Test and take on board the insights of the early 'modern magical astrologers' like the English Qaballists, who found that – approached appropriately – solar conjunctions were extremely potent for particular kinds of magic, rather than entirely counter-productive.

Lastly, don't be in too much of a darned hurry, what you are working with is TIME, one of the most potent forces in the magical universe, so learn slowly and thoroughly. In fact, with magical astrology as with many areas of magic, it is more important to be able to **unlearn** quickly than to learn fast.

That's my introductory rant done; I hope it is useful, it is certainly impartial, which is more than you will get in a lot of other places!

ASTROLOGY FOR GOLEMS

Crowley may be getting a bad name nowadays, but some of his work was genuinely useful. Included under this heading is his very short and to the point instruction on 'How to construct a figure of the heavens' which manages in a couple of pages to communicate effectively what others do badly in entire books. As setting up a chart is the first major hurdle to becoming informed about astrology, one can always add refinements later. I include said instruction here, taken from *The Complete Astrological Writing*, pp. 27-29:

It is a very easy matter to set up a figure of the heavens suitable for astrological judgement. [...] The first thing to be done is to provide yourself with an Ephemeris [...]. The present generation of astrologers employ that issued by 'Raphael' and we shall suppose the student to possess it. At the left hand of the left hand page will be found the date and the day of the week. Pick out the day which you require.

In the next column is given the Sidereal Time. We need not here enter into what that means. We merely give the rule. If the hour and minute for which you set up the figure is for afternoon, add that hour and minute to the Sidereal Time for the day. If it be before noon, find out how much before noon, by subtracting the hour and minutes from twelve hours (thus eight o'clock in the morning is four hours before noon) and subtract the result from the Sidereal Time. If, in the first case, the time obtained is more than twenty-four hours, subtract twenty-four hours from it. In the second case, if the time before noon is greater than the Sidereal Time, add twenty-four hours to the Sidereal Time. You then turn to the end of the book and look at the Tables of Houses for the place for which you wish to set up the figure.

Now, take the blank form with which you have provided yourself, a circle divided into twelve parts. At the top of the Tables of the Houses you will see the Sidereal Time marked on the left-hand side. Run your eye down the column until you find the nearest approximation to the new Sidereal Time which you have made by adding or subtracting the hours as stated above. Now, against the house in your blank figure which is marked ten, put the sign and degree which is given in the column next to the Sidereal Time in the Table of Houses, and fill in the others as far as the third house accordingly. From the fourth house to the ninth no figures are given, and it is not necessary that they should be given, for the fourth house is equal and opposite to the tenth, the fifth to the eleventh and so on. Thus if 16 Cancer be on the cusp of the tenth, 16 Capricornus will be on the cusp of the fourth. […]

You then proceed to insert in this figure [the chart] the planets in their proper places. For example, suppose 24 Virgo is on the cusp of the eleventh house, and you find the Sun marked as in 22 Virgo, you put him slightly in front of the cusp; if in 26 Virgo slightly behind it. The daily motion of the Sun is always within about 3 minutes of a degree and it is, therefore, quite unnecessary to make any calculations depending upon the hour of the horoscope. […] We then consider the position of the Moon; the Moon's daily motion is very large; it is sometimes as much as 15 degrees or even a little more. It is sometimes as low as 12 degrees or even a little less, but this works out approximately as a degree every two hours. In the Ephemeris, the [lunar] positions for both noon and midnight are given. You should take noon or midnight according to whether the hour of the horoscope is nearer the one or the other. By allowing half a degree an hour you will get the Moon's position [approximately and close enough to] correct [...]. Thus suppose the time you want is 9 o'clock in the evening and the Moon at midnight on that day is 8 degrees, 37 minutes of Taurus [...] subtract a degree and a half, which will give you 7 degrees of Taurus. You then go on to the right hand page of the Ephemeris, which gives you the positions of the other planets.

I've snipped remarks on the Moon's Nodes and on relative motions of the planets. It is only necessary to take a little care with Venus and Mercury – who though fast are appreciably slower than the Moon – and then only if super accuracy is required, which it rarely is.

However, these instructions are not much abbreviated here and compared to many manuals are extraordinarily concise, permitting the student to set up a chart with minimal confusion, particularly for locations covered by the short Table of Houses in the back of *Raphael's* ephemeris – a larger book of Tables is also available from *Raphael's* which greatly extends the range. It should be noted that the format of *Raphael's* ephemeris has slightly changed since Crowley wrote. Larger ephemerides with data for fifty years at a time are available, but the outlay for a *Raphael's* ephemeris for one year is so minimal as to be a useful recommendation for our 'starter kit'.

For most purposes, including rite timing, when it comes to plotting aspects the 'Ptolemaic' ones are almost all that is really needed: conjunct, opposition, sextile, square, and trine. The only exception is inconjunct/quincunx (the name differs depending which side of the Atlantic the astrological books were written), which does seem more important than other minor aspects not occurring in Ptolemy's writings. (These are divided into 'hard' aspects: conjunct, square and opposition; and 'soft' aspects: the sextile and trine. Two of the former are 'malefic' and the latter 'benefic', but it is principally hard aspects that cause events, with soft aspects making for benign influences and outcomes.)

Following these instructions, you can set up a chart, which is usually the biggest obstacle to beginning the study of astrology. One of the benefits of astrology, as opposed to other occult arts, is many of your friends and acquaintances will be willing guinea pigs for you to hone your skills on. Indeed, you should immerse yourself in practice as well as research, and keep the charts you have done for clients formal or informal for reference. Later you may wish to refer back to an individual chart, or examine trends in connection with certain aspects across several of your 'case studies'. This observational work is an important part of astrology, and part of how it continually updates itself, something most critics of the art – or of Tropical Astrology in particular – fail to appreciate. One hesitates to suggest that this is because their position is theoretical and abstract, and the astrologer's art is essentially practical and applied in the real world.

Even though astrology is a thoroughly traditional part of magical practice, it has rarely featured in modern occult primers. Separating magic and astrology however is an artificial modern affliction, preventing both from fully reinvigorating themselves, or indeed each other. Earlier I presented this book as necessary in the wake of various changes since the previous crop of established primers appeared. Adding astrology to the existing format is no bad thing and serves several germane purposes, not least of which is further exploration of the decans in more Greco-Egyptian forms, or as connected with early demonology rather than GD/AC forms. Continuing and deepening this area of the new landscape, as it were, will require astrological skills, or at least familiarity with the language, in order to participate or appreciate.

This represents a purpose for astrological skills at primer level in present magic, but they are also necessary for tasks too long neglected, which I hope to see undertaken in future. Prominent among these, scarcely beginning to unveil themselves in our era, but replete with nocturnal and zoomorphic magic demanding exploration and new life, are the Lunar Mansions.

THE LUNAR MANSIONS

[W]hen any star ascends fortunately, with the fortunate aspect, or conjunction of the Moon, we must take a stone, and herb that is under that star, and make a ring of the metal that is suitable to this star, and in it fasten the stone, putting the herb, or root under it; not omitting the inscriptions of images, names, and characters, as also the proper suffumigations.

Agrippa TBOP I.47, p. 40.

The Lunar Mansions have been an interest of mine for a great many years. As with most subjects of that description, modern occultism was oblivious to them for much of that time, and my sources have necessarily been academic ones primarily – not that this has stopped me experimenting with them in various ways, not even remotely. Meanwhile, it has been suggested I should start by telling the reader what they are. This in itself is problematic in a strict sense, as they are ancient and have undergone changes and redefinitions in different periods and by various cultures and practitioners. It is even a matter of dispute where exactly they come from, although India has an excellent claim and the old idea that anything astrological had to be 'Chaldean', or at least Mesopotamian, has very little to support it in the case of the Mansions.

So, let us approach it another way. How can we usefully define them, and why should we be interested? This is easier by far. Like the Zodiac and the Decans, the Mansions are a division of the heavens into equal parts, in their case, twenty-eight. We could argue over how the original division was made, agonise over what the start-point was first considered to be, and so forth. However, interesting such questions can be, historically speaking, introducing the Mansions handily and emphasising practical use in modern magic requires another approach. What is needed for our purposes is an immediate handle on them to enable engagement and access to the advantages they confer. In particular, this handle should be readily compatible with Western traditions like the Tropical Zodiac assumed or employed throughout Agrippa, the grimoires, and beyond. From here, things get much easier.

Thus, the cycle of the Mansions may be conveniently commenced at the Aries Equinoctial point, and measured from there, as well as commencing any series of 'attributions' at the same place. It is simple enough for emerging specialists to experiment with alternatives once facility is gained. This arrangement has long been part of the background of both 'Agrippan' grimoire magic and traditional Western astrology and is thus readily combined with 'grimoire improvisation', to coin a phrase. Also noteworthy is the assimilation of the Mansion cusps within William Lilly's astrology, as 'Critical Degrees'.

In each of the Cardinal Signs, at whose commencement in the year the Equinoxes and Solstices occur, three Mansions have their beginning: at 0 degrees, 12° 51' 26", and 25° 42' 52" in each case. In each of the Fixed Signs, two Mansions have their beginning 8° 34' 18" and 21° 25' 44" for each as before, and for the Mutable Signs also two Mansions, commencing in all cases at 4° 17' 10" and 17° 18' 36". For convenience, the end of each Mansion is regarded as the same point as the beginning of the next, thus:

1. ♈ 0 degrees	8. ♋ 0 degrees	15. ♎ 0 degrees	22. ♑ 0 degrees
2. ♈ 12° 51' 26"	9. ♋ 12° 51' 26"	16. ♎ 12° 51' 26"	23. ♑ 12° 51' 26"
3. ♈ 25° 42' 52"	10. ♋ 25° 42' 52"	17. ♎ 25° 42' 52"	24. ♑ 25° 42' 52"
4. ♉ 8° 34' 18"	11. ♌ 8° 34 18"	18. ♏ 8° 34' 18"	25. ♒ 8° 34' 18"
5. ♉ 21° 25' 44"	12. ♌ 21° 25' 44"	19. ♏ 21° 25' 44"	26. ♒ 21° 25' 44"
6. ♊ 4° 17' 10"	13. ♍ 4° 17' 10"	20. ♐ 4° 17' 10"	27. ♓ 4° 17' 10"
7. ♊ 17° 18' 36"	14. ♍ 17° 18' 36"	21. ♐ 17° 18' 36"	28. ♓ 17° 18' 36"

A little facility with tracking the daily movements of the Moon – in the ephemeris if not the heavens – will soon enable following her course through the Mansions. The next thing to consider is the relation of the Mansions to the stars and constellations. There are two matters to take account of here: firstly, the Mansions were always closely related to the stars and may be employed as a framework for working with them magically; secondly, while Agrippa, the *Picatrix*, and other sources employ the pattern tabulated above, the stars mentioned in connection with them have moved significantly since those texts were composed.

EXAMPLE STAR POSITIONS, AGRIPPA VS PRECESSION

AGRIPPA POSITIONS	PRECESSED POSITIONS
Aldebaran 3° Gemini	Aldebaran 9° 38' Gemini
Sirius 7° Cancer	Sirius 13° 57' Cancer
Procyon 17° Cancer	Procyon 24° 24' Cancer

This certainly accords with some conceptions of the Precession of the Equinoxes marking changing rulerships per astrological age, as different stars rise at the beginning of the seasons and so forth. Thus, Tropical Astrology does not ignore such changes; plotting stellar movements within its frame clearly delineates them! However, the technical implications and mythic and demonological aspects of this are generally ignored, through no fault of the system itself. This I propose to address, and supply tools for putting it into operation.

In other words, current use of the mansion frame has to work with the stars as and where they are now, not how they were then. This is one area where working 'by the book' is demonstrably redundant, and there is no alternative but to reformulate. Thus, my account is necessarily designed with improvisation and experimentation in mind, while historical materials have been relegated to appendices for purposes of illustration and reference. The Moon, representing changefulness and mutability, is more than suited to such an approach.

Many of the stars listed later in this work are associated with the Mansions traditionally. This includes, but is not limited to, the fifteen Behenian stars whose sigils and other details Agrippa (TBOP) gives in somewhat dispersed form across several quite separate chapters. However, I have included stars not in the 'Path of the Moon', a course not identical with the solar zodiac, and already breaking rules of declination, though not so much as the decans. My justification is that the mansion frame is a useful and appropriate handle on Fixed Star magics in general. This includes some stars far distant from the Ecliptic but long associated with magic, and relatable to specific degrees of the Zodiac, and thus to mansion spaces. I accept, endorse, and uphold Ebertin's premise that distance from the ecliptic is not in itself a limiting factor, and wish to encourage experimentation along those lines. Also included are one or two Southern stars, not visible in Northern climes; this for similar experimental reasons and to assist bringing the art forward from its 'Chaldea-centric' past.

Technically a couple of points are enough to start with. Firstly, some astrologers are resolute that any star more than 23 degrees from the Ecliptic – the band of the solar zodiac – has no technical use. The fact that the decans were originally defined by stars which do not conform to this rule is reason enough to doubt its applicability in magic, not to mention the well documented cults of circumpolar stars. All that is required is that the longitude of a star may be referred to the Zodiac, regardless of its declination, a point Ebertin also makes in his manual in regard to Natal Astrology. That this is true of magical astrology besides is at very least an intelligible experimental proposition, one confirmed in my own practice and testable in yours.

Next, ritual elements may be found elsewhere in this book, but the astrological approach is essentially this: time your ritual to coincide with an applying conjunction of the star in question with one or more of the 'personal' factors in the chart, particularly the Moon, the Ascendant, or the Midheaven, for example, Moon conjunct Spica ascending or culminating. The Orbs for conjunctions given here are very conservative; more generous ones may be found in natal manuals and could be worked with, but generally as close an aspect as possible is to be preferred. One might also work with planetary conjunctions to the Fixed Stars, but the Sun in particular should be avoided. Such an aspect is termed 'combustion' and swamps the energy of the star. My teacher in astrological magic expressed this as the Sun turning the energy of the body combusted to universal purposes, whereas we seek to turn that energy to personal results.

This outline of the 'rule' is very skeletal, and other factors may be tied in as the experimenter gains a foothold in astrology and becomes familiar with the mansion framework. That it likely breaks all manner of 'classical' or Renaissance rules of magical astrology need not deter us. The complexity and sophistication of Electional Astrology is not for everyone, nor can we always wait for the best chart. This is a down and dirty, readily applied technique which has the added virtue of being easily repeated on a regular basis, in the maintenance of a talisman for example.

CONTEXT AND ORIGINS

HECATE AND THE DACTYLS IN THE PAPYRI

In the Greek Magical Papyri (PGM LXX. 4-25) is a ritual plainly drawing on a background of Mystery cult practice. The ritual has been the subject of a paper by the editor Hans Dieter Betz, whose analysis of the rite places it in the late third or early fourth century CE, and he identifies elements of a catabasis ritual from the Mystery cults in it. This initiation involved both Hecate and the Idaean Dactyls, as at Samothrace. As appropriate for a catabasis ritual, the rite involved a descent into a cave. This of course is comparable to that of Trophonios, of necromantic oracles, and even the grotto of Mithras. It is also germane to recall that the Idaean Dactlys are the 'Greek' equivalent of folklore's metal-working dwarfs, reputed teachers of Orpheus, founders of the Mysteries, the first to work iron and the first to bear the titles of 'goetes' (wizards) in the ancient literary record (see *Geosophia*).

The ritual in the papyri meanwhile is a charm against fear of punishment in the Underworld. This alone should alert us to its eschatological background. There are many interesting details in the ritual, not least two authentic protective magical gestures from the period. Two brief formulae precede the rite (PGM LXIX. 1-3 and PGM LXX 1-4) wherein similar protective formulae are contained. The first advocates saying PHNOUNEBEĒ twice, then 'give me your strength, IO ABRASAX, give me your strength, for I am ABRASAX', the entire formula to be repeated seven times, while holding your thumbs. The second, which may be fragmentary, introduces itself as a charm for favour or protection by undoing a hostile spell, further describing itself as a phylactery and a charm for victory. While similar in purpose, the words recited differ from the above: 'AA EMPTŌKOM BASYM, protect me'. The ritual in question then follows, and in the introduction the ritualist is instructed to identify themselves with Ereshkigal (in this period seen as identical with Hecate, as becomes apparent) who is 'the one holding her thumbs', referring to the same gesture used above. The magician or initiate uses this formula when confronted in the Underworld by a chthonic spirit. If 'he' (the spirit) approaches after the performance of the above formulae and gesture, then the magician performs another magical gesture, taking hold of their right heel. An additional formula follows, being a recital of Hecate's symbols: virgin, bitch, serpent, wreath, key, herald's wand, golden sandal. These are plainly symbols of a Mystery rite and recur throughout the papyri.

Another part of principal interest to Betz, and very relevant to us, involves a further recitation. This includes a variant of the 'Ephesian letters' and a declaration that the ritualist has been initiated, has descended into the underground chamber of the Dactyls and seen the sacred things (the symbols of Hecate aforementioned). The location envisaged for this adventure is a crossroads, which while it may also represent an earthly place, is nevertheless synonymous with that in the geography of Hades. The instructions that follow are specific: having performed this, turn around and flee (that is, do not look back as you depart). The context has changed and similarly the gender of a potentially dangerous spirit changes. It is in such places, the text avows, that 'she' appears, and it is clear that 'she' is Hecate.

There follows an additional and presumably related application; reciting this formula late at night, concerning whatever you wish, and the rite will cause it to be shown you in dream. Another, darker, application then follows; recite it while scattering sesame seeds should an Underworld entity lead you away for death and it will preserve you. This occasion could equally be when visiting the

Underworld as a 'shaman', or in the post-mortem state as an initiate possessing special knowledge.

These formulae all regard manipulation of the Underworld, even though the applications apparently differ. A further ritual then follows, and again Hecate theology is clearly discernible; shape a cake from best quality bran, sandalwood, and the sharpest vinegar, and write the name of your intended victim on it. While doing this the operator looks into a magical light while saying the name of Hecate (likely this indicates the recitation of the appropriate formula: PHORBA PHORBA BRIMŌ AZZIEBYA), adding a request to deprive the target of sleep. Although such instruction is missing, it is clear enough that the intention is that the cake forms a ritual deposit at a crossroads. Its resemblance to a cake for Cerberus, as well as the general context of the material collated, makes this a clear inference. Further protective formulae follow, one of which involves speaking through two knives, reminiscent of the magical use of swords in Balkan rituals with a similar Mystery cult background.

This collection of protective formulae is extremely interesting and underlines various facts. The ASKEI KATASKEI formula is, as we would expect, attributed to the Dactyls; unusually the author also refers to it as 'the Orphic formula'. This, in my opinion, does not and cannot imply that this is an invocation of Orpheus, an interpretation made by Georg Luck in *Arcana Mundi*. Rather it simply conforms to the ancient idea that the rites of the Dactyls came under the tutelage of Orpheus; or as we might say, the Orphic movement.

On a practical level, it is plain that both this formula and the recital of the symbols of Hecate – from an authentic initiation ritual – are here magical devices for protection in a variety of underworld contexts. So too, the leaving of the site without looking back conforms to both the myth of Orpheus, and the magical preparations made by Jason for obtaining the Golden Fleece. Plainly,

these are authentic and widely known gestures and practices, worthy
of our attention in the modern context.

The symbols previously listed occur in a variety of contexts
in the papyri, of which one is particularly interesting (PGM VII.
756-94). Throughout these fascinating texts a female and lunar
form appears, balancing the male solar-pantheistic deity (Abraxas,
Helios, Aion, etc.). In this particular rite appears a list of 14 sounds
and 28 symbols. Their number implies multiples of the seven vowels
of the Greek alphabet and of the seven planets corresponding. Of
the 28 symbols, 21 are animals, the last 7 reproduce the symbols
above mentioned. The terms of the incantation reveal that the deity
addressed is essentially 'lunar-pantheistic'. Only IAO who made
her is higher in nature; she is 'mistress of the whole world'.

OTHER PGM REFERENCES

This concept, of 28 sounds and symbols ruled by the Moon as
parts of a magical astrological worldview, also appears in PGM
XII. 253-54:

Yours is the eternal processional way [of heaven], in which
your seven-lettered name is established for the harmony of
the seven sounds [of the planets] which utter [their] voices
according to the 28 forms of the moon.

Important traces of a lunar magical technology appear
elsewhere in the papyri. They are worth detailing here, both to
underline the conceptual importance of the rituals just described
and to introduce elements resonant with what is to follow.

In PGM V. 370-446, concerning the making of a magical
image of 'Hermes', we are instructed to 'take 28 leaves from a pithy

laurel tree and some virgin earth and seed of worm-wood, wheat meal and the herb calf's-snout', with the aside that a 'certain man of Herakleopolis' takes '28 new sprouts from an olive tree' iinstead. So, this method evidently has variants, suggesting reasonable distribution and common use. The image itself is made by pounding together the foregoing ingredients with the liquid of an ibis egg made into a uniform dough and fashioned into a figure of Hermes wearing a mantle, while the moon is ascending in Aries or Leo or Virgo or Sagittarius. It should be noted that these are the three fire signs plus Virgo.

The spoken component of the ritual contains several significant phrases underlining its relation to the 28 sounds and symbols of Hecate, here syncretised with Selene, goddess of the Moon:

Hermes, lord of the world, who're in the heart,
O circle of Selene, spherical
And square, the founder of the words of speech,
Pleader of justice's cause, garbed in a mantle,
With winged sandals, turning airy course /
Beneath earth's depths, who hold the spirit's reins,
O eye of Helios, O mighty one,
Founder of full-voiced speech [...]

Regarding the Lunar Timing in the above, note also PDM Suppl. 168-84, concerning an incantation for a 'god's arrival' (*phntr*, an important technical term originating in the Egyptian sphere prior to Hellenisation). Reminiscent of the previous instruction, the 'day on which you will do the god's arrival' is while the moon is in Leo, Sagittarius, Aquarius (is Aries intended here?) or Virgo.

Such references as these reinforce the impression that Virgo has a privileged role in the lunar timing of the papyri, in no uncertain terms; viz: PGM III.275-81 and PGM VII. 284-99. In the first of these we are told regarding the lunar 'Horoscope' — i.e. the sign rising with the Moon — that

> in [...] Virgo: anything is obtainable, perform bowl divination, as you wish; in [Cancer]: perform the spell of reconciliation, air divination...; in Gemini: perform spells of binding...; [in] Libra: perform invocation... spell of release... necromancy; in Pisces... OIŌ or love charm; in Sagittarius: conduct business /...; [in] Capricorn: do what is appropriate; in...

The second, in similar vein, and in more complete form reiterates that with

> Moon / in Virgo: anything is rendered obtainable. In Libra: necromancy. In Scorpio: anything inflicting evil. In Sagittarius: an invocation or incantations / to the sun and moon. In Capricorn: say whatever you wish for best results. In Aquarius: for a love charm. Pisces: for foreknowledge. / In Aries: fire divination or love charm. In Taurus: incantation to a lamp. Gemini: spell for winning favour. In Cancer: phylacteries. Leo: rings or binding spells.

It is worth noting that not only does Moon in Virgo enable any kind of operation, but in both cases the entire listing begins with Virgo, rather than, say, Aries. Interestingly, Virgo also commences Chinese formulations of the Lunar Mansions, wherein Spica is regarded as the special star of spring, called Kio, the Horn.

THE MANSIONS AND THEIR SYMBOLS

The 28 symbols and their physical analogues, such as laurel or olive leaves, are effectively correspondences of the Lunar Mansions, which I have elsewhere taken the liberty of attributing to the conventional Mansions of the grimoire tradition, with some additions. As the last seven symbols differ from the remainder insofar as they are not animal symbols, I have also collated animal symbols from other related rites of the papyri to supplement them. The attribution is a convention facilitating work with the individual Mansions. The reader need have no fear that I have made errors in this attribution. Lunar animals are essentially interchangeable, and there is no correct order; four groups of seven such animals would do equally well, following the precedent of other lunar rites. In theory one might even employ one lunar animal – a cat, say – for every single Mansion. What I give here is simply a system with resonance in the earliest part of the tradition, with the potential advantages implied by individual symbols linked to core tradition. I refer the reader to the account of things considered 'lunary' in Agrippa (TBOP 1.xxiv) where a major list of animal symbols occurs, in which appear beasts, fish and fowl associated with the Mansions, and indeed the decans as their derivative:

...all kinds of Dogs; the Chameleon; Swine, Hinds, Goats; Baboon; Panther; Cats; the Civet-Cat; Otters, and such as prey upon fish; Mice; Geese, Ducks, Didappers, all kinds of water fowl as prey upon fish, as the Heron; Wasps & Bees; small Flies and Beetles; but most Lunary of all is the two-horned Beetle horned after the manner of a Bull: which digs under Cow-dung, and there remains for the space of twenty eight days, in which time the Moon measures the whole Zodiac, and in the twenty ninth day, when it thinks there will be a conjunction of their brightness, it opens the dung and casts it into Water, from whence then come Beetles. Amongst fish these are Lunary, catfish [*Bagre marinus*]; the Tortoise, the Echeneis, Crabs, Oysters, Cockles, and Frogs.

LUNAR ANIMALS FROM PGM

Ox	Wolf*	Baboon	Mare
Vulture	Serpent**	Cat	Bitch
Bull**	Horse	Lion	She-wolf
Scarab	She-goat	Leopard	Cow
Falcon**	Asp [OR Royal Uraeus]	Field mouse	Camel
Crab*	Young horned goat*	Deer	Dove
Dog	He-goat*	Dragoness	Sphinx

* Agrippa's 'Lunary Animals'
** indicates Dodekauros

Prominent modern magician Aleister Crowley too had an interest in lunar symbolism; in his writings he frequently refers to 'Yesod' as the Treasure House of Images. This interest explains, I feel, the prominence of particular animals in his 'Holy Book', *Liber VII*, which I feel is worth tabulating here in a form I have previously employed as an alternative to the PGM list.

LUNAR MANSION CUSPS	SYMBOL FROM THE PAPYRI (SEE ALSO LIBER VII & LXV)	ANIMAL SYMBOL FROM LIBER VII (SUGGESTED)
0 Aries	Ox	Fawn
12 Aries	Vulture	Centaur
25 Aries	Bull	Horse
8 Taurus	Scarab	Rabbit
21 Taurus	Falcon	Fox
4 Gemini	Crab	Phoenix
17 Gemini	Dog	Goat
0 Cancer	Wolf	Worm
12 Cancer	Serpent	Satyr
25 Cancer	Horse	Bull
8 Leo	She-goat	Elephant
21 Leo	Asp [OR Royal Uraeus]	Tortoise
4 Virgo	Young horned goat	Oyster
17 Virgo	He-goat	Osprey
0 Libra	Cynocephalus Baboon	Pelican
12 Libra	Cat	Cow
25 Libra	Lion	Scorpion
8 Scorpio	Leopard	Hound
21 Scorpio	Field mouse	Snake
4 Sagittarius	Deer	Hawk
17 Sagittarius	Polymorph [Dragoness]	Fish

0 Capricorn	Virgin. Mare	Cicada
12 Capricorn	Torch. Bitch	Wolf
25 Capricorn	Lightning. She-wolf	Tiger
8 Aquarius	Garland. Cow	Sparrow
21 Aquarius	Caduceus. Camel	Ibis
4 Pisces	Child. Dove	Serpent
17 Pisces	Key. Sphinx	Camel

The association of the Mansions with 'Ara'' astrology is a misnomer; the Arabs are here, as elsewhere, the heirs of the Hellenistic synthesis. The question remains, from where did the Greeks obtain them? Earlier scholarship has shown that they are not Chaldean in origin. Assuming a civilisation rather than a nomadic origin, the most likely original source appears to be India, which had a lunar astrology from the period of the Vedas. It is important to recognise that this lunar reckoning could measure a year as well as a month and involved stellar observation for that purpose. As Weinstock (LMEC, p. 54) points out:

In the Vedic literature a certain phase of the Moon in a certain constellation is often mentioned, for instance, 'full moon in *phalguni*' (= 9th mansion, in Leo): as this happens only once a year this dating is not less correct than that given by the rising of a star.

From these earlier Indian origins, in Late Antiquity they were adapted to Hellenistic astrology and thus to the modern Western tropical schema, which I propose to employ. Tropical Astrology with its zero Aries point is not the only system for working with the Mansions, but for the purposes of modern synthesis, it is the most straightforward; it dovetails with the grimoires and with modern astrology in a coherent fashion. I therefore make no apologies for not working from the Indian 'sidereal' system, which while valid in its sphere lacks the syncretic qualities which I consider desirable.

The question of historical precedence need not really detain us much further. Our knowledge of the Greek structure is partly inferred from the papyri, the *Codex Cromwellianus* and other Arab but ultimately Greco-Indian derived material. What is needed are some consistent modern models extrapolated on traditional lines. Thus, for example, this fragment of a Chinese mansion system given by Weinstock (LMEC, p. 63) is instructive:

No.	CHINESE MANSION NAME	PLANETARY RULER	ANIMAL SYMBOL
1.	Kio	Jupiter	Dragon kiao
2.	K'ang	Venus	Dragon
3.	Ti	Saturn	Badger (?)
4.	Fang	Sun	Hare
5.	Sin	Moon	Fox
6.	Wei	Mars	Tiger
7.	Ki	Mercury	Leopard
8.	Teou	Jupiter	Unicorn
9.	Nieou	Venus	Ox

Here, as with other more Western schemas, the planetary rulers of the Mansions are listed in order of the Days of the Week, 4x7=28. These are, so to speak, the Days of Creation rather than our 'earthly' days: the week is simply a frame or 'holding pattern' which is most natural to a lunar system. In Chinese tradition it is natural that Jupiter (ruler of Thursday) would commence the cycle; he is after all the patron of their sixty-year calendar system, with its own Zodiac, or 'Circle of Animals'. In conventional Western magic such a symbolic Week might commence with Sunday, or with Saturday (see table below). For our modern syncretic purposes however, I propose a Monday start-point, consistent with the *Grimoire of Honorius*, but with more extensive ramifications. Essentially the case is that a Sunday start-point to a Decan system would not surprise us, and a Monday start-point to the Mansions is as natural. Both Sun and Moon are rulers of Time (*kronocrators*), and indeed each has Saturnine associations of their own accordingly with this. What we are seeing here, and why I have taken such a long way around the subject, is a system proper to the 'lunar pantheistic deity' (Hecate), and a handle on a methodology for which a combined historical and practical study is obviously required and deserved. This is necessary to balance the much clearer picture available regarding the 'solar pantheistic' (Helios Apollo) side of the tradition, with the potential to achieve far more than that is hopefully visible by this point.

PLANETARY RULER SCHEMATA

LUNAR MANSION CUSPS (LILLY'S 'CRITICAL DEGREES')	PLANETARY RULER (CHALDEAN ORDER)	PLANETARY RULER (DAYS OF THE WEEK, TRADITIONAL)	PLANETARY RULER (PROPOSED, SEE ABOVE)
0° Aries	Saturn	Sun	Moon
12° Aries	Jupiter	Moon	Mars

25° Aries	Mars	Mars	Mercury
8° Taurus	Sun	Mercury	Jupiter
21° Taurus	Venus	Jupiter	Venus
4° Gemini	Mercury	Venus	Saturn
17° Gemini	Moon	Saturn	Sun
0° Cancer	Saturn	Sun	Moon
12° Cancer	Jupiter	Moon	Mars
25° Cancer	Mars	Mars	Mercury
8° Leo	Sun	Mercury	Jupiter
21° Leo	Venus	Jupiter	Venus
4° Virgo	Mercury	Venus	Saturn
17° Virgo	Moon	Saturn	Sun
0° Libra	Saturn	Sun	Moon
12° Libra	Jupiter	Moon	Mars
25° Libra	Mars	Mars	Mercury
8° Scorpio	Sun	Mercury	Jupiter
21° Scorpio	Venus	Jupiter	Venus
4° Sagittarius	Mercury	Venus	Saturn
17° Sagittarius	Moon	Saturn	Sun
0° Capricorn	Saturn	Sun	Moon
12° Capricorn	Jupiter	Moon	Mars
25° Capricorn	Mars	Mars	Mercury
8° Aquarius	Sun	Mercury	Jupiter
21° Aquarius	Venus	Jupiter	Venus
4° Pisces	Mercury	Venus	Saturn
17° Pisces	Moon	Saturn	Sun

LUNAR CORRESPONDENCES INTEGRATING ELEMENTS OF THE MAGICAL
PAPYRI AND THE TRUE GRIMOIRE

Animal symbols in brackets are extrapolated from elsewhere in the
papyri to give 28 animal symbols, as explained previously.

LUNAR MANSIONS CUSPS/ CRITICAL DEGREES)	ANIMALS AND SYMBOLS FROM THE PAPYRI	GRIMOIRE SPIRITS
0 Aries	Ox	Lucifer
12 Aries	Vulture	Syrach*
25 Aries	Bull	Satanachia
8 Taurus	Scarab	Agliarept
21 Taurus	Falcon	Fleruty
4 Gemini	Crab	Belzebuth
17 Gemini	Dog	Sargatanas
0 Cancer	Wolf	Nebiros
12 Cancer	Serpent	Astaroth
25 Cancer	Horse	Scirlin*
8 Leo	She-goat	Claunech
21 Leo	Asp [OR Royal Uraeus]	Musisin
4 Virgo	Young horned goat	Bechaud
17 Virgo	He-goat	Frimost
0 Libra	Cynocephalus Baboon	Klepoth
12 Libra	Cat	Khil
25 Libra	Lion	Mersilde
8 Scorpio	Leopard	Clisthert

21 Scorpio	Field mouse	Sirchade
4 Sagittarius	Deer	Hiepact
17 Sagittarius	Polymorph [Dragoness]	Humots
0 Capricorn	Virgin [Mare]	Segal
12 Capricorn	Torch [Bitch]	Frucissiere
25 Capricorn	Lightning [She-wolf]	Guland
8 Aquarius	Garland [Cow]	Surgat
21 Aquarius	Caduceus [Camel]	Morail
4 Pisces	Child [Dove]	Frutimier
17 Pisces	Key [Sphinx]	Huictigaras

LUNAR MANSIONS CUSPS/ CRITICAL DEGREES)	PLANETARY RULER (PROPOSED, SEE ABOVE)	LUNAR WEEK RULER FROM HONORIUS
0 Aries	Moon	Lucifer
12 Aries	Mars	Nambroth aka Frimost
25 Aries	Mercury	Astaroth
8 Taurus	Jupiter	Acham aka Silcharde
21 Taurus	Venus	Bechet aka Bechard
4 Gemini	Saturn	Nabam aka Nebirots (2)
17 Gemini	Sun	Aquiel aka Acquiot
0 Cancer	Moon	Lucifer
12 Cancer	Mars	Nambroth aka Frimost
25 Cancer	Mercury	Astaroth

8 Leo	Jupiter	Acham aka Silcharde
21 Leo	Venus	Bechet aka Bechard
4 Virgo	Saturn	Nabam aka Nebirots (2)
17 Virgo	Sun	Aquiel aka Acquiot
0 Libra	Moon	Lucifer
12 Libra	Mars	Nambroth aka Frimost
25 Libra	Mercury	Astaroth
8 Scorpio	Jupiter	Acham aka Silcharde
21 Scorpio	Venus	Bechet aka Bechard
4 Sagittarius	Saturn	Nabam aka Nebirots (2)
17 Sagittarius	Sun	Aquiel aka Acquiot
0 Capricorn	Moon	Lucifer
12 Capricorn	Mars	Nambroth aka Frimost
25 Capricorn	Mercury	Astaroth
8 Aquarius	Jupiter	Acham aka Silcharde
21 Aquarius	Venus	Bechet aka Bechard
4 Pisces	Saturn	Nabam aka Nebirots (2)
17 Pisces	Sun	Aquiel aka Acquiot

*Syrach and Scirlin are alter egos: essentially as Scirlin he is the intermediary for the hierarchy, as Syrach he is a chief within the hierarchy. The only practical complexity around this is that when invoking Syrach one calls upon him as Scirlin first, as with the other spirits.

THE LUNAR MANSIONS AND THE BLUE GRIMOIRES

> The Rosicrucians are a People I must bring You acquainted
> with. The best Account I know of them is in a French Book
> called *La Comte de Gabalis*, which, both in its Title and Size, is so
> like a Novel, that many of the Fair Sex have read it for one by
> Mistake. According to these Gentlemen the four Elements are
> inhabited by Spirits, which they call *Sylphs, Gnomes, Nymphs,* and
> *Salamanders*.
>
> *The Rape of the Lock*. Alexander Pope (1712, p. xii)

My original intention when composing this part of the book was
simply to clarify a *modus operandi* based on the Lunar Mansions and a
particular spirit catalogue, an open-ended approach I have evolved
over many years and can recommend as a modern route into
exploration of the Mansions as a magical model. The *Night School*
project has had ideas of its own, however, and has sent me off on
various journeys 'processing' ideas in unfamiliar locations and from
new angles, and indeed embedding the necessity of doing so within
this book. Thus, after some lapse of time working 'in the dark' as
regards the intentions of my Muse, I was presented with another
option entirely. In short, I planned to approach the subject of the
Mansions via a blue grimoire adapted to the purpose (or latent or
implicit within it?), only to be presented with a Lunar Mansion
schema explicitly embedded in another one. What this may say
about the composition of the other, or indeed of undetected factors
within the genre as a whole, is an open question. To be perfectly
clear, an association of the *GV* spirits with the Mansions may have
pre-existed my connecting the two.

Meanwhile, with both the planned and the unplanned examples herein, there is a *dramatis personae* and a star catalogue already linked or linkable to the lunar cycle as represented specifically by the Mansions – but in what appear to be two entirely different ways. Appearances, however, can be deceptive.

The first has an 'established" spirit catalogue which gives formal discipline to the pattern by anchoring it in tradition, plus a star catalogue, which by contrast is not written in stone but a combination of traditional marker stars and others of magical interest collated for the purposes of experiment and exploration with the aforesaid anchor. The spirit catalogue is of course that of the *True Grimoire* and its relatives, updated here in line with the latest research but otherwise much as I have employed it in the past. The core group so to speak are readily and simply 'corresponded' with the Mansions, and various practical applications are facilitated by doing so. While apparently 'synthetic', it appears to match something quite archetypal, and the structure has more subtleties than may appear at first glance.

The second case is more complicated, in some respects, and simpler in others. It has been encountered by some of my readers before, in the *Testament of Cyprian the Mage* – to be specific, the catalogue of spirits from the *Heptameron* or *Magical Elements* attributed to Saint Cyprian (a book quite distinct, it should be said immediately, from the *Heptameron* of Pietro d'Abano). At the time I referred to this catalogue as resembling lists of spirits of the Decans, as in the *Testament of Solomon*. In fact, Decan and Mansion attributions and uses are not dissimilar, and subsequent research shows quite clearly that it was Mansions that were intended, give or take some idiosyncrasies.

At that time, I had, as implied, no intention of revisiting the grimoire, but fate and the muse had other ideas. A correspondent from abroad contacted me with news that I could not ignore. I had mentioned in various places that the names of the Elemental

Rulers in modern magic – Djin, Nicksa, Paralda, and Ghob – had not so far been traced further back than Eliphas Levi. It has now become apparent that the *Heptameron* material, which does name them, precedes him, by at least a few years, and also that there are mysteries concerning the country of origin, date, author, and sources of said material. There are, to clarify, duplicates of its material in another work which are more complete than the published version I worked from.

This is the *Petit Manuel du Devin et du Sorcier* by Nathaniel Moulth, which I first took for a pseudonym, disguising an author of which nothing is currently known beside what he reveals of himself in this work. More recently a feasible identity of his astrologer grandfather (Thomas-Joseph Moult without a final 'h', 16th-century author of *Prophéties Perpétuelles*) was discovered, but Moulth himself remains mysterious. Inquiries at the National Library of France revealed that they know nothing of him other than his writing this work, regarding which, it has long been an adage of mine that if you do not know what your sources were reading, you do not know your sources. Knowing what Nathaniel Moulth was reading enables us to know not just something about him; it clarifies and reveals the genre in which he wrote, and the ideas current amongst such authors.

THE GOSPEL ACCORDING TO NATHANIEL MOULTH

In order to promote both brevity and clarity, the subject of the 'blue grimoires' requires a swift reintroduction, assuming either an existing background knowledge or willingness to acquire it. Pre-eminent in and emblematic of the entire genre are two works: *Le Petit Albert* and the older *Grand Albert*, which while originating earlier than the period of the 'Bibliotheque Bleue' acquired greater distribution and status during it. The works are distinct, but share certain qualities, among them being the incorporation of texts and fragments from a variety of older sources. The genre contains various conjure manuals such as *Le Dragon Rouge* (the 'blue' successor to the *Grand Grimoire*), cheap editions of the *Grimoire of Pope Honorius*, and of course the *Grimorium Verum*. In recent years these have benefitted from renewed attention unspoiled by class distinctions previously obscuring the importance of the genre. The two *Alberts* – which are equally deserving of the title 'grimoire' – have as yet not received so much attention as these, a situation that now requires address.

There are various elements in both that are contextually important to the whole evolution of the genre and the worldview involved with the conjure manuals. There is a relation, too, between various manuscript grimoires and the 'Albertine' world, and it can be misleading to view contemporary manuscript production and the publishing phenomenon as entirely distinct occurrences. A minor aspect of this relationship was covered – and employed – in my *Sworn and Secret Grimoire*, wherein grimoire scribe Frederick Hockley was shown to be familiar with *Le Petit Albert*.

The Albert of the title is Albert the Great, although another figure has also been conflated with him, and this ascription must be seen as emblematic rather than serious. Several of the collated texts found in both works can be attributed to other later authors, and no serious effort at forgery is involved. Also, there is nevertheless a serious relation between the works and older Books of Secrets associated with Albertus Magnus. So, it is relevant to have a term describing these and related works, and since it is left to me, I propose Albertine, rather than Albertian.

Among the features of these works that should be briefly mentioned, and perhaps clarified, are such things as palmistry and other divinatory arts surrounding the body, such as reading moles and lines on the face. These often accompany chapters on astrology, of varying quality, and frequently connect with the planets. While I do not propose a major examination of these – some relevant allusions may be found in *TCM* – it is important to place them in context. This focus on the human body as exhibiting astrological qualities and energies in physical form is undoubtedly part of the worldview of the later grimoire genre. While its manifestations in these arts may have spurious elements, the thinking behind it is very much in the here and now of physical life, compatible both with post-Paracelsian thought and our sublunar model.

Brevity was mentioned, and presently the relevance of the Albertine grimoires is specific rather than general. They can be shown to have been a solid part of Nathaniel Moulth's worldview, their themes, at his fingertips, familiar enough to improvise from and employ creatively, a textual tradition possessing implications he could draw from.

Item one, an illustration from the 1895 edition of the *Grand Albert*. I propose that this example of our popular title is unlikely to be the first edition carrying this plate and there is no pressing need to pursue the matter. More relevant to our theme, I propose that Nathaniel Moulth was rather familiar with an *Albert* carrying this plate; although equally he may have been in a position to add it to contemporary editions himself. While the frontispiece of this edition claims Latin antecedents in 1651, we need not look so far for the original engraving of the illustration. In 1796 Constantin François de Chassebœuf, Comte de Volney, published *The Ruins: Or a Survey of the Revolutions of Empires*. Therein, among other things, he sought to demonstrate, as various rationalist and humanist thinkers were to do subsequently, that the biblical account of Christian origins was not historical, but myth built on an astrological foundation – a basis shared, according to this argument, with the pagan theologies that had preceded it.

A VIEW OF THE ASTROLOGICAL HEAVENS OF THE ANCIENTS TO EXPLAIN THE MYSTERIES OF THE PERSIAN, JEWISH, AND CHRISTIAN RELIGIONS.

Plate II.

FROM VOLNEY'S *RUINS, OR MEDITATION ON THE REVOLUTIONS OF EMPIRES.*

True or false, this was a learned and respectable work by a recognised academic. It appeared firstly in French, and swiftly if subsequently in English with the patronage of then Presidential hopeful Thomas Jefferson and the American Philosophical Society. Volney's *Ruins* is the original abode of the plate; various details or components of which appeared as subsequent illustrations elsewhere in the text – and very likely in Moulth's visual imagination. The quality of the plate varies between French and English editions, but the dependence of *Le Grand Albert's* plate on Volney is very apparent. One might go so far as to suggest Volney's *Ruins* was the kind of book that publishers and composers of blue grimoires had on their shelves. Incidentally, in Mary Shelley's *Frankenstein*, Volney's *Ruins* is the first mentioned of the books the Monster finds and educates himself with.

Item two, the illustrations of astrological talismans in *Le Petit Albert*, themselves derived from Paracelsian sources if not directly from the man himself. These – complete with embedded references to gnomes guarding treasure mirrored directly in some Solomonic MS texts, **and** the *Prayer of the Salamanders* – are among the more interesting elements of the work, and Moulth was as familiar with them as with the astrological plate mentioned previously.

The talismans of Moulth's *Manuel* are in fact elaborations on the Albertine originals, providing a practical modus operandi for working an astrological magic of the Mansions, with a theoretical and mythic cosmology directly involving the plate from the other *Albert*. Among other details, Moulth elaborates on the identities of the Greco-Roman gods originally depicted, to include Hecate, and Egyptian gods Horus, Isis, Typhon, and Osiris as alter egos. Three of these Egyptian names also appear on Volney's plate. I should also draw attention to the inscription accompanying Virgo in the above image, and also to its position.

MOULTH'S TALISMANS AND THE GODS

Alchemy […] is the office of Vulcan…
On The Errors and Labyrinth of the Physicians, Paracelsus

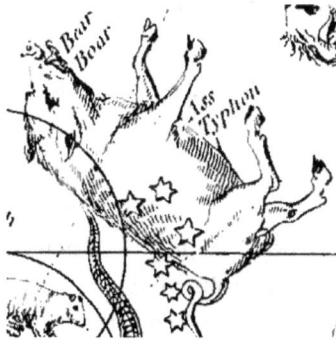

Moulth's handling of the talismans of the *Petit Albert* involves adaptation, in the form of 'Sanskrit' characters for writing the names, and in the names themselves. Rather than the names of the Roman gods of the days, he is inclined to substitute other, more startling ones. On occasion he even repurposes the talismans altogether, for example, when invoking Paralda his talisman bears the name Hecate in Sanskrit characters and a number square on the back. This suggests routes for our own adaptations of the planetary images and squares for works with individual Lunar Mansions and their spirits. Regarding the use of a magical alphabet for such work, if desired, my recommendation would be to employ the 'Paracelsian' Alphabet of the Magi (see page 56) instead.

c   i,j,y   th   h   z   u,v   e   d   c   b   a

t   s   r   k,q   ts   f,p,ph   o   x   n   m   l

The material as he gives it is characterful and eccentric at points, but requires some abbreviation in presenting it here, thus for example, on his Saturn talisman, the name Saturn is replaced with Typhon:

Seal of Saturn. Its metal is lead, his day Saturday, and his hours 1st, 8th, the 15th and 22nd. Its magic square is of three bands and its mystical number is 15. Its polygon has nine equal sides. Its symbolic figure represents time armed with its formidable scythe, in the attitude of a man who mows, with an hourglass next to him; sometimes it's an old man with a long beard, stooping over a burial pit that he seems to dig with a pickaxe. On his head is a star, and, at the top of the talisman, the word Typhon, written in Sanskrit characters. Making the talisman must end when Saturn is in favourable aspect. The moon entering the first degree of Taurus or Capricorn. When the plate is finished, wrap it in a piece of black cloth. This talisman helps women in childbirth and gives them birth without much pain. It also brings prosperity in all things. If a rider puts one in his left boot, his horse will not be hurt. However, it produces the opposite effects, as do all such talismans, if done in circumstances where aspects are bad or unfavourable.[1]

OTHER GODS

Basilides had taken from the word abracadabra the name of God or Abraxas, whose mystical symbol, dear to the Egyptians, was Osiris or the sun. Now, remember that, my dear neophytes, because what I am going to tell you has never been revealed. Jehova, Dies, Abraxas, Osiris and Unity, holy Unity, are the five names of the great architect

---

1 Nathaniel Moulth, *Petit manuel du devin et du sorcier, contenant le traité des songes et visions nocturnes... l'art de tirer les cartes, [...]*, (Paris: Passard, Libraire-Éditeur, 1859), pp. 470-471.

of the universe, united all the greater and marvellous as it is composed of a triad: Osiris, omnipotence; Isis, creation; and Horus, wisdom.[2]

His solar talisman includes an image virtually identical to the *Petit Albert*'s:

Seal of the Sun. The purest gold is its metal. His day Sunday, and his hours on the 1st, 8th, the 15th and 22nd, one and eight o'clock in the evening, three o'clock and ten o clock in the morning [sic]. So it is on Sunday, and at only those hours you can work at your talisman. You take the pure gold, and you make a round plate, the thickness you think proper, smooth on both sides. You first draw a circle all around this plate in order to make it perfectly round, and in this circle you enter a polygon which will have as many equal sides as there are units in the magic square you draw in the polygon. We call a magic square, a square divided into several small squares forming bands, and filled with the terms of an arithmetic progression, which are so arranged there those of the same band or the same row, both in length and in height and in diagonal, added together, give the same product. Here is the magic square of the sun which will serve as an example.

---

2 Moulth, *Petit manuel*, p. 496.

6	32	3	34	35	1
7	11	27	28	8	30
19	14	16	15	23	24
18	20	22	21	17	13
25	29	10	9	26	12
36	5	33	6	2	31

Since there are six units in this magic square, the square will be enclosed in a hexagon. When a band is added in total, it will constantly give the number of 111, because this number is that of the big stars which are under the domination of the sun [sic] and who owe their influence to him. Each planet, as we will see later, has a fixed number of stars which are subject to it in the same way, and this number, such as it is, is that of their square magical. In the arcs formed on the circle by the sides of the polygon, you place the angels of the planet, that is to say the signs of the zodiac in the which it is most pleased. So, he is enthroned in the lion; at Sagittarius he is a friend of Jupiter; he gets excited and enjoys with all his might in the Ram [the three fire signs]. You will do as much for the seal of the other planets.

On the other side of the plate, you will engrave the sign of the planet, which represents a crowned king, seated on his throne, holding in his right hand a scepter with which he cows a lion. his head is the radiant image of the sun, and, in the Sanskrit characters, the name Osiris. What makes this talisman very rare and very difficult to make, is

that, for it to have all its power, it is necessary that the last
stroke of the engraving, either that you engrave it yourself
if you have the talent, either have it engraved before
your eyes and at your place by an artist, it is necessary,
I say, that the chisel stroke which ends the work is given
positively when the sun is in conjunction with the moon
when entering the first degree of the lion. You then wrap
the plate in a piece of yellow cloth, which is the color of
the sun.

This talisman puts you in touch with all the powerful
of the earth, kings, princes and great lords, whose
benevolence and favors it makes you obtain. It makes you
appreciate everything, and overwhelms you with riches
and honours.[3]

His Seal of Jupiter also follows the imagery of the *Petit Albert*,
being made of tin, on a Thursday, in the hours of Jupiter. The
square is the familiar one of four bands. He encloses it in a polygon
of nine sides. The image is not the kingly Jove of the *Grand Albert*,
but a priestly figure holding a book, often associated with Jupiter
elsewhere.

Above his head is a shining star, and above this the word
Horus, in Sanskrit characters. We have to complete the
talisman the instant the appearance of the planet is
favorable, when the moon enters in the first degree of the
sign of the scales, when the sun inhabits the crayfish, or the
sagittary or the fish. As soon as we have finished wrap the
plate in a piece of sky-blue cloth.[4]

---

3 Moulth, *Petit manuel*, pp. 461-463.
4 Moulth, *Petit manuel*, pp. 467-468.

The Seal of Venus follows similar lines, made of copper on a Friday in the hours of Venus. Seven bands, and a polygon of nine sides, while the image remains that of:

> … a scantily clad woman, holding a lute in her left hand, and having her right resting on the head of an Eros having bow and quiver on her back, and a flaming arrow in his hand. The woman is wearing a star on the head, and above it is written the word Isis, in Sanskrit characters. We will finish the talisman when the planet is in the sign of Taurus, the moon having entered the first degree of the sign of bull or virgin. We wrap the plate in a piece of green cloth.[5]

We are given similar instructions regarding the Moon, whose talisman 'is made absolutely like that of the sun, and its polygon is also hexagon, but its magic square is nine bands of numbers.

---

5 Moulth, *Petit manuel*, pp. 468-469.

On the other side of the medal will be engraved the image
of the planet, which is a woman wearing a dress ample and
broadly draped: her feet are on a crescent, a star on her
head, and a crescent on the left hand. The word Hecate
will be written above, in Sanskrit.

The operation should be done in the spring, when
she is in the first degree of Capricorn or Virgo, with a
favourable aspect of Jupiter or Venus. When it is finished,
we wrap it in a piece of white cloth.[6]

It will be noted that the figure given earlier of a Hecate talisman
associated with Paralda does not have the ample and broadly
draped attire described here. Plainly the repurposing of planetary
talismans for Mansion work need not necessarily employ the same
name, image, or even number square as the prototypes.

The Seal of Mercury corresponds to Wednesday, and the
hours are the those of Mercury. Its metal is fixed mercury,
which is fixed as we said previously. Its cabalistic square is
of eight bands and its polygon has nine equal sides. He has
his throne in the Virgin, his power and strength in Virgo and
scales; his exaltation in the Virgin only, and, in the Ram, he
is loved by Mars. His cabalistic image represents a genius
with wings on his back and heels and holding a caduceus
in his right hand. He has on the head a star, and above, the
word Hermès written in Sanskrit characters [Mercure, or
Mercury is the form in the Albertine grimoires]. We will
complete the talisman the instant Mercury enters one of
the favourable houses that we have just indicated, when it
is in a favourable aspect. When the talisman is finished,

---

6 Moulth, *Petit manuel*, p. 465.

you wrap it in a piece of purple cloth. He has the property of making discreet and eloquent, which is very useful for young people in love; he helps wonderfully in the study of science, and makes the memory strong; he cures fever, and finally, if we put it under the bedside, it provides prophetic dreams.[7]

The Seal of Mars. Mars' day is Tuesday, its hours on the 1st, 8th, 15th and 22nd; his metal is iron. We will therefore use the best iron that one can obtain, and one will act absolutely as for the preceding talismans. The cabalistic number is 65, and the square is five bands. His throne is in the scorpion; his joy in the Virgin, and his exaltation in the Capricorn; but his strength and power are in the scorpion and the ram, and Mercury is his friend. Its polygon must have nine equal sides. The mysterious figure will present a warrior armed from all parts, the left hand leaning on a shield, and the right hand holding a drawn sword. He has a star on his head, and above it the name of Mars written in Sanskrit.

The chisels and other tools that will be used to make this talisman be new and well soaked, and that it be finished when the moon is in good aspect with some other planet, and when it enters the first degree of the sign of the Ram or Sagittarius. We wrap the plate, when it is finished, in a piece of red cloth, and not in white canvas, like the previous ones [sic]. Whoever wears it with faith and respect will be invulnerable in battle, and always victorious, in addition to greatly increasing his strength and courage. If it is buried under the ramparts of a strong city or a citadel, the place cannot be stormed. But, if the talisman was made when

---

7 Moulth, *Petit manuel*, pp. 466-467.

Mars is in opposition to the favourable planets, it brings bad luck.[8]

Figures des 7 Planètes pour graver sur les Talismans de Paracelse

Moulth is also familiar with the conceptions of Elementals set forth in the *Comte de Gabalis*. Indeed, he is, as one might say, a good Paracelsian in terms of his source material and general worldview. His half serious, half tongue in cheek approach shares much with *Gabalis;* with such erudition, intentions are likely less frivolous than sometimes appears with both. In fact, *Gabalis* is also

8 Moulth, *Petit manuel*, pp. 465-466.

the likeliest source for the Salamander prayer in *Petit Albert*, where interestingly it is recommended for placating gnomes, neighbours of the Salamanders in this sublunar Paracelsian ontology. *Gabalis'* conception of the Sylphs is also assumed or known in several such books, including an earlier *Manuel*. Our introductory account thus summarily set forth, a return to the spirits of the grimoire will doubtless be welcomed. Here too our author may be known by his reading habits. Though the fact is never openly stated, his spirit catalogue is undeniably collated in large part from the works of Sir Walter Scott. Interestingly enough, elsewhere Moulth does mention "Lord Byron, Walter Scott, and so many other famous lame people (*célèbres boiteux*)" while discussing the First House in Astrology, which among other things represents oneself. Is it possible that Moulth too walked with a cane, like these other sons of Vulcan?

THE SPIRIT CATALOGUE OF THE *PETIT MANUEL*

The People of your World became so dull and stupid, that my Companions and I lost all the Pleasure, that formerly we had in instructing them: Not but that you have heard Men talk of us; for they called us Oracles, Nymphs, Fairies, Household-Gods, Lemmes, Larves, Lamiers, Hobgoblins, Nayades, Incubusses, Shades, Manes, Visions and Apparitions.

Cyrano de Bergerac,
The Other World: The Comical History of the States and Empires of the Worlds of the Moon and Sun, 1657, p. 36.

Where the *Heptameron* gives spirit names, sigils, and some oddly incomplete connections with stars, this form of the material includes those but is also more forthcoming and complete as regards the latter. Let us begin with an examination of the chiefs of spirits.

SPIRIT CHIEFS	STAR FROM MOULTH	DEGREE AND NAME, ETC.
Beelzebuth	Antares	Alpha Scorpius, Cor Scorpionis, 09° 46' Sagittarius.
Baalberith	Zeta Cancer	Tegmine: 1° 21' Leo
Queen Niksa, chief of Undines	Gamma Aries	Mesarthim, 3° 11' Taurus

King Gob (Ghob elsewhere), chief of Gnomes	Zeta Cancer	See Baalberith.
Queen Paralda	Alpha Virgo	Spica. 23° 51' Libra
King Djin	Sirius	Sirius 14° 05' Cancer

At first glance there may appear to be problems with this attribution. To begin with, two out of six chiefs appear to be attributed to the same star. Perhaps too one might expect the so called Four Persian Royal Stars to figure somewhere (say Aldebaran Earth, Regulus Fire, Antares Water, and Fomalhaut Air), but neither Regulus nor Fomalhaut appear anywhere in the entire attribution. However, our expectations might legitimately be suspended, and internal consistency sought rather than matches with *a priori* notions.

Nonetheless, these stars most certainly appear in traditional mansion patterns and deserve close attention. Paralda's star, Spica, for example, is far and away the most benefic Fixed Star of all. The star associated with Nicksa, Mesarthim, once marked the Spring Equinox and is known in Manzil, Nakshastra, and Sieu traditions (Arab, Indian, and Chinese mansion systems respectively).

Tegmine, associated with Baalberith and with Ghob here, closely mirrors my attribution of *Verum* spirits to the Mansions, since the intermediary Scirlin aka Syrach corresponds here. Antares is certainly properly represented too, so that we might wonder if Aldebaran should appear here – as Ghob's star perhaps – rather than elsewhere in the system. However, again, there is plenty of viable practical material to take further as things stand. Indeed, Tegmine's dual correspondence is likely structural rather than an error.

Accordingly, these additional positions, extending the data available when writing *TCM*, are recommended as worthy of attention. Finally, note carefully how the context in which these names are embedded differs from the more usually encountered 'sanitised' modern form of these elemental rulers. They are revealed here in their full goetic glory: Four Kings and Queens of the twenty-eight Mansions of the Moon attended by their elemental demon cohorts.

The material as a whole is not unproblematic; indeed, it is markedly eccentric, is not of the early generations of grimoires but of fairly late vintage, and has to be approached from several angles to evaluate properly – a process still in the earliest stages. Nevertheless, its literary, astronomical, and magical conundrums and conceits conceal something useful, if we exercise our 'freedom of belief' and explore it sympathetically.

We have lost a great deal of material relating to the Mansions, and much that remains, from Agrippa and the Arabs, is semi-obsolete due to precession. Here, in a more recent but obscure source (or sources, the back history is still to be fully explored through the older grimoires) we find an approach semi-adapted to modern times. As has been shown in my *True Grimoire*, such more recent sources can sometimes provide useful stepping-stones towards archaic approaches associated with far older source works.

The material obtained via Moulth is evidently either the original source or at least closer to the source than the Cyprianic *Heptameron*. The same remarks about the reliance on Sir Walter Scott's works in compiling the spirit catalogue apply but it occurs at an earlier stage of transmission. This 'pre-*Heptameron*' material has better spellings and clarifies identities in several cases, extending the visible reliance on Scott. Vitally, it also names the stars with which these spirits are associated, a very major omission in the *Heptameron*. It is very clear contextually that this is an omission, and the attributions are not a subsequent addition. The *Heptameron* says that they correspond to stars, and even classifies them as good or bad; it simply does not give their names, and the text reads oddly as a result in places. The account each gives of the upper hierarchy of spirits however is essentially identical:

MOULTH: these are the names of the leaders of the six legions of geniuses and dark spirits, with whom magicians can enter into direct communication.

HEPTAMERON: The six signs that are in this table are the black names of the heads of the six legions of geniuses and spirits, with which we can enter in direct communication.

Beelzébuth commands all the demons.

Léonardo [Leonard, who also has the alias Baalberith] presides over Sabbats under the dark figure of a black goat.

Numbers 3, 4, 5, and 6 are the names of four chiefs of geniuses who serve most the designs of men; they preside over the four elements of the Arabs.

Nicksa; The queen of the waves, and they that inhabit the sea and great lakes

Gob [Ghob]; the chief of the gnomes; that inhabit the bowels of the earth, & keep the metals and occult treasures

Paralda; the queen of the sylphs; they that inhabit the air

Djin; the chief of the salamanders, who live in the fire; their main occupation is casting metals, causing the volcanoes

If Moulth is not the ultimate source, which is not proven, he is nevertheless drawing on the same material as the *Heptameron* but transmits it in more complete form and has to be considered prior.

There are peculiarities present, and it is possible that yet older versions still to be examined have differences, but the core of the material is readily 'generalised' and tabulated; from whence various analytical tools can be brought to bear.

All this aside, this spirit hierarchy has certain more or less obvious features. First and foremost, it places the Elemental Kings and Queens in a goetic context, also – as will be further shown – a Sabbatic one. The chief of the spirits is none other than Beelzebuth, as in the *Testament of Solomon* and other venerable older texts and grimoires. It is a quirk of demonology, whether grimoiric, literary or – frequently – religious, that distinguishing between, for example, Lucifer, Belzebuth, and Satan is either arbitrary or dependent on context. Beelzebul in the *Testament of Solomon* identifies himself with the planet Venus, which tends more to identify him with Lucifer. They are often distinguished in spirit catalogues, so when comparing systems things can seem a bit awkward when one is preferred over another as Chief of all. That neither Lucifer nor Astaroth nor yet Satan are included for completeness in our text need not concern us; a single 'Maioral' figure and a 'Trinitas' are effectively interchangeable anyway, a consideration making practical interaction between such systems easier. Moulth however provides a more colourful explanation:

> 1, is the sign of Beelzebub, who is currently reigning after having dethroned Satan; according to Berbiguier [he is] the exterminator of the sprites. He commands all demons...[9]

Meanwhile, it should be reiterated that this goetic and Sabbatic aspect of his source, clearly, is not carried over by Eliphas Levi in his (re)presentation of the Elemental Kings and Queens (see both *Rituel de la Haute Magie* and *Sanctum Regnum*). His discussion of the rulers

---

9 Moulth, *Petit manuel*, p. 424.

and the Elementals imposes the North/Earth, South/Fire, East/Air, West/Water pattern, which, while resembling later approaches, as does his use of drawn pentagrams and hexagrams, need not be considered reliable. Even less so is his confusion of the Cardinal Signs (which imply a very different elemental/directional spread), where he supposes Aquarius to be watery, and 'the Eagle' (Scorpio) to be Air. In short, despite his reputation, his 'angelicisation' of Moulth's material is tangential and posterior.

BAALBERITH AND THE SABBAT

When Baalberith, their prince – best known to witches under the name of Leonard – traverses the air, every wizard who meets him greets him with a lot of respect and makes salutation to the prince.

Nathaniel Moulth, 'The Sabbat', (PMDS, p. 504)

Moulth's text is more specific than is the *Magical Elements* that Leonard and Baalberith are two names of one spirit; the odd duplication of the upper hierarchy in the *Heptameron* does not occur here. Nevertheless, perhaps we should not dismiss its suggestion that Leonard presides over the Sabbat, and Baalberith over dreams and dreamers, despite their evident identity. There are, for instance, several spirits of the *GV* who are concerned with dreams and sleep, and there are historical threads connecting dreamers and witches, some important Italian ones included.

From Moulth's description of the Sabbat, we learn that Baalberith (aka Leonard) is usually the chief VIP present; as it were delegating for 'Satan', whose appearances are less frequent. I have remarked before that the various descriptions of 'Leonard' are an exact match for woodcut representations of Lucifuge Rofocale (in both *TCM* and *Pandemonium*). In the hierarchies of the *Grand Grimoire* with 'forerunners' of the *GV* we find that Lucifuge and Syrach (Syrachi, Scirlin) hold the same position in their respective, evidently related hierarchies. Their equivalence is all but a given of comparative examinations of these texts.

The immediate practical inference of these identifications is that Baalberith, in the Moulth and Cyprian text at least, has the role of 'messenger/minister' or 'intermediary spirit'; intermediary, that is, between the Chief (Belzebuth) and the Four Elemental

Rulers: Paralda, Nicksa, Ghob, and Djin; and has shared authority
over their subordinates. His importance in practical sorcery and in
evocation, or conjure magic, is evident from this. Now, to provide
a taste of the flavour of our author, Nathaniel Moulth, and of his
spirits, I present:

THE SABBAT

All I can reveal to you on the Sabbat is that which we
have learned from the revelations of the sorcerers. They
were tortured to extract from them the confession and the
details of their crime. Also from the trial of the unfortunate
Gaufridi, who was burned alive as a sorcerer, which only
proves that his judges were not.

To be admitted to the Sabbat one must have made
a pact of alliance with the devil; having sold one's soul
in exchange for riches, or for supernatural power, all for
a number of years. The bargain occurs in the crossroads
of a forest, or in the old ruins of an abandoned castle at
midnight; all amidst the deepest darkness.

The devil usually appears under the form of a mature
man dressed in black or in red, hiding his hoofs in wide
shoes, and with two small horns under thick black and
curly hair. Some witches have clarified, being put to the
torture, that he would be a very good-looking man if he
did not have a big wart on his nose, which disfigures him
a lot. Other times he appears in the shape of a great black
goat with golden horns, and a horn-bell with a wooden
clapper hung at his neck. But it seems he does not take this
form only to preside over the Sabbath.

Before he appears, the recipient must summon him.

For this he begins by drawing around him, with a stick of hazel picked in the clear of the moon on the eve of the day of the dead, a great circle magical that the curious crowd of demons cannot cross to torment him. After drawing this circle, he recites the following abominable words:

Rector universalium qui resplendes in inferno, Invocatur nomen tuum Baalberith, praevaleat imperium tuum, compleatur lex tua, sicut in inferno et in terrâ.

[Universal Guide that art resplendent in hell, I invoke thee in thy name Baalberith, your kingdom overcomes, your law is completed, in hell as it is upon earth.]

So the aspirant in devilry lights a brazier of iron and when the charcoal of cypress, boxwood and rosemary are ardent, casts upon it a perfume composed of fat from an unbaptised child, pure sulphur, asphalt, vervain seeds and black henbane, of black cat's blood, and hearts of male toads, taken in a cemetery. As soon as the reddish smoke begins to rise in the air, the wind roars in the ruins and through the trees of the forest: the owls and bats flit around him by sounding their cries and their funereal whistling; a thousand fantastic ghosts, lamias, larvae, lemurs, manes, spectres, ghosts and werewolves move menacingly around the magic circle, and make incredible efforts to penetrate it. The storm increases and becomes a veritable tempest, which breaks and uproots the trees and shakes the old edifice even to its foundations; the piled clouds loose a thousand livid lightnings, by the light of which the recipient perceives distinctly the whole hellish court of Satan, dancing as one around the magic circle.

Then the neophyte of the devil utters these hideous words:

Fomentum desideratum concede credentibus et postulantibus hoc die: et abstergas nobis facinora nostra, sicut nos favemus maleficientibus.

[Foment the desires and grant the requests of your believers; and wipe away our crimes, as we smile maleficently.]

As soon as he has finished, the storm stops, the demons disappear, and the devil appears in flesh and bones next to him in the circle. There, they amicably agree the conditions of their pact, and the bad spirit, after writing it in characters of the Grimoire, on a parchment made with the skin of an excommunicate, has the recipient sign it with his blood. When all is done, Satan takes away his glove and applies his infernal seal, that is to say one of his claws, to the skin of the new wizard, in any part of the body, and this application produces absolutely the same effect and the same pain as a red-hot iron. The skin remains a blackish brown in this place and loses forever its sensibility. Here you can embed a needle or a punch, without the sorcerer experiencing the least pain. This mark is what the courts called the seal of the devil, and it was the sign by which judges recognized the wizards they burned. One Perkins [William Perkins, theologian and theorist on witch proofs 1558–1602; here perhaps confounded with Matthew Hopkins] had such skill finding this mark on the most secret parts of the body, that he alone delivered to the courts, who burned them, more than fifty wizards and witches, within six months.

The devil, having completed the pact, gives the recipient the information necessary to attend the next Sabbat that will be convened. He learns also that to get there conveniently, he just has to rub the body with an ointment consisting of absolutely the same drugs of which he made his perfume of invocation.

As I said, we find most of the facts I have recounted in the procedures of wizards who were burned. Also in the statements of Miss Mandols [Madeleine de Mandols, accuser and witness, herself tried for witchcraft forty years later] in the Gaufridi case. We have from our former neighbor, the famous invocator Berbiguier from Terre-Neuve du-Thym, who has been dead for two or three years, some details that we thought we should add to this article. Sorcerers do not know, or at least most of them, on what day will be held the assembly of the Sabbath. They are called there by the trumpet of the devil, which is a cornet à bouquin [a medieval wind instrument, also called a cornett, cornetto, or zink].

But the sounds of this infernal cornet, albeit spread through the whole universe, can be heard only by the sorcerers. So, everyone sets out to get there by the shortest route and the least tiring, which is through the air. The women, generally, to make the journey more convenient ride on a broomstick. as M. Victor Hugo very well said.

When Baalberith, their prince – best known to witches under the name of Leonard – traverses the air, every wizard who meets him greets him with a lot of respect, and makes salutation to the prince.

The Sabbath is always at night, in a solitary place, in a forest clearing, near a crossroads, especially if it has a gibbet, and it has been noticed that the grass does not grow again in the place where it was held. Sometimes, however, the place of the assembly can be underground, or in ruins, or a vast cavern, and often an old, abandoned church. The room is lit, if it is in an old church, by candles composed of pitch and sulfur; if the assembly is rural, it is illuminated by luminous snails that roam the leaves of bushes and nearby trees, which produces a lot of effect, and by the flaming eyes of big toads that come to attend and sit at the diabolical banquet.

Upon arrival, each sorcerer and witch begins by paying homage to the prince or rector presiding over the assembly, because it is not always Satan in person; most often he gets replaced by Baalberith, in the form of a goat. This tribute goes in a singular way: the goat turns his behind, lifts up the tail, and the kneeling wizard kisses him... where you guess! Then they greet the princess, his wife or his mistress, who has the peculiarity of having two forms at one and at the same time. With the populace of the lesser sorcerers, she has a black face, inflamed eyes, a flat nose, and a disproportionately large mouth, always open, always smoking; but in the eyes of the prince and wizards of distinguished rank, she is always of ravishing beauty.

At the Sabbath, the great occupation consists of hexes, and instructing newcomers in the art of composing evil charms, to cast evil spells, etc., and the old wizards share this occupation with the devil. For recreation, they have fun imitating the ceremonies from the church and ridiculing them. Then comes the moment of the feast. Telling you what you eat there would be a terrible thing, and yet we had a fatal sample no more than two years ago, at the cemetery of Montparnasse, and another fifteen or so years ago at Fontainebleau.

The dishes that are served on the Sabbath have the special peculiarity of never satiating the guests. Knives, because they can be placed cross wise; salt, because it is the symbol of wisdom; oil, because used in some religious ceremonies, are severely excluded from this banquet.

When the president judges that the orgy has sufficed in duration, he makes his horn bell clink. Everybody arises and hastens to remove planks of old coffins to make the table. The wizards and witches, bare as an ungloved hand, are caught by their hand and dance a dishevelled round, while the devil plays the bagpipes. The infernal dance only halts for more frantic, more abominable debauchery. This awful scene lasts until the break of day, or earlier when the cock has crowed. As soon as the echo of his voice is heard, the demons and the wizards, frightened by its magical impact, flee and disappear, along with the last traces of their terrible feast.

If, in order to gorge on human blood more readily, some wizard or witch left the Sabbath to roam the countryside in the form of a werewolf and throw themselves upon travelers and children astray in the night, at cockcrow they resume their natural form. They can, sometimes, be devoured by the real wolves, in whose company they had put their self to devour the remains of his victims.

I would never finish if I were to tell you everything concerning the Sabbat and sorceries, going from the procedure of Gaufridi to others of the same kind. I merely point out to you that all these revelations were made under torture. If some testimonies agree it is so the victim, exhausted by constantly renewed pain (the ordeal being repeated thrice of four times to those who retracted), could end it at the stake.

And now, my dear neophytes, I have educated you in magical and cabalistic sciences and more. If you practice my lessons, and especially if you get all the results that we promise, you can boast of being more learned than the deepest Magi. I will not be jealous of it, and I will not seek to belittle your talents, as do some teachers of secular science.[10]

---

10 Moulth, *Petit manuel*, pp. 501-507.

PARALDA, LUNAR TALISMANS, AND THE BEHENIAN STARS

The four elements are, it is said, populated by spirits called sylphs, gnomes, nymphs, salamanders. Gnomes are the demons that dwell in the earth and are very evil spirits. Water is the residence of nymphs, as fire is that of salamanders. As regards the sylphs which are spread in the air, these are the prettiest and kindest creatures in the world. It is easy to have commerce with them, under a certain condition, which, in truth, is not suitable for everybody: it is to be excessively chaste.

M. Comte, *Nouveau Manuel Complet des Sorciers*, (1853)

Let us now meet the central character of Moulth's mytho-
magical narrative, the Queen of the Sylphs, brightest star in the
constellation of Virgo, 'friend of the Sun and of Hecate'. There
can be no doubt whatsoever that Moulth identified Queen Paralda
(leader of the Sylphs or Sylphides) with the central figure straddling
the spheres of Ormazd and Ahrimanes, of Summer and Winter,
Good and Evil. The implicit symbolism – an intermediary between
worlds, including, naturally, the Underworld below the horizon and
our daylight world – could scarcely be clearer. He is drawing on
'Age of Reason' themes regarding an alleged 'Unity of Religion' (in
Volney's *Ruins*) but equally he is drawing, as seen, on the Albertine
grimoires, in one of which at least this same plate appears. This
could, and probably should, be taken as reflecting the manner of
thought of some grimoirists and grimoire compilers of the time. As
we have seen, many of them include allusions to themes in *Gabalis*
and Paracelsus, as well of course to the *Prayer of the Salamanders*.
Some commonalities of thought among them may fairly be assumed
more likely rather than less. Incidentally, the *Prayer* is employed by
the *Petit Albert* in placating the Gnomes specifically. The idea that
there needed to be a prayer for all four kingdoms does not arise until
Levi. He had divested the four rulers of their original context, and
utterly changed their character. I have no qualms about reversing
this entirely, since so many matters of interest neglected by post-
Levi ceremonial magic are involved, the Lunar Mansions being a
major one, though by no means the only such; several blind spots
in our understanding of the grimoires, their predecessors, and their
spirits are illuminated too.

Whether everyone can easily grasp the idea that a Queen of an
Elemental Kingdom can be portrayed as a near, or actual, divinity
is neither here nor there. This is plainly what Moulth does, and the
image on page 81 helps explain how non-eccentric this is. The Four
Elements first arise in ancient literature in the work of Empedocles.
His Elements are undoubtedly ruled over by four divinities, and,

while attributions vary, one of them is traditionally associated with this same constellation, namely Nestis, also called Persephone. Her myth also involves transiting between worlds, that of her husband Aidoneus or Hades – also an Empedoclean elemental ruler – and that of Zeus and Hera, the two others. I have discussed this aspect of the Elemental theme in detail elsewhere, but the point is clear enough.

There is a great deal more, some signalled by the 'legend' adjacent to her image. The names Eve and Isis are natural enough, indicating various directions in syncretism. While not diminishing these in the least, the name I wish to point to – picturing us together in a planetarium with a revolving Volneyian celestial sphere projected on the ceiling – is Sybille.

Here again, a guide between worlds is evoked, in the form of the Sybil of Vergil's epic poem, the *Aeneid*, itself often viewed as a magical text. We should say, evoked first, since Paralda Queen of the Sylphs also bears more than a passing resemblance to the 'Fairy Queen' of various grimoires, Sybillia. So too, obscure references to Sybilline magic occur in both the *Arbatel* and *Abramelin*; the Christian *Arbatel*'s relationship with the myriad kinds of magic it lists, bearing classical Greek and Roman titles that are utterly pagan, might be considered ambivalent but provocative. *Abramelin* is more dismissive, which is to say, unilluminating; however, the other texts and traditions its author sneers at include recognisable and important names and texts. Reginald Scot's *Discoverie of Witchcraft* is much more forthcoming, giving us an English conjuration of the Sybil clearly resembling other rites where her name is omitted (the spell for causing three ladies to appear in your room, found in the *GV*, is only one such among many. Some forms increase the number to seven). This later genre identified, the earlier phase of it to which *Abramelin* likely refers are partly illuminated by our modern access to the *Hygromanteia* and associated traditions. Here we meet another important 'stand-alone' female spirit, Sympilia,

and a probably related Kāle, the Lady of the Mountains, who
sports a Melusine-like tail in one manuscript. Both are evoked in
rituals essentially separate from 'collective' spirit catalogues, as
the figures in the above-mentioned rites are. Any notion that the
ritual in the *Grimorium Verum* was selected for its novelty founders
on the evidence of a continuous and meaningful theme rooted in
ancient Underworld mythology, powerfully perpetuated within
both folk and grimoire traditions. My only problem with the *GV*
form is its suggestion of adaptation to make gentlemen rather
than ladies appear if the operator be female, which while probably
well-intentioned obscures the real purpose of the ritual. There is
of course nothing whatsoever to prevent female practitioners from
working with the Sibyl and her sisters.

Meanwhile, the coherence of Moulth's material should also
enliven us to the seriousness beneath his occasional rationalising
banter, his literary moods or their targets, and his misdirection. His
'spirit catalogue' presents us with strong coherent themes. Rather
than being less serious than – say – the forever-referenced catalogue
of Johann Weir, his presents us with forward looking adventures into
territories part obscured, part revealed. I have presented various
materials related to these themes throughout the Encyclopedia
Goetica, often to incomprehension where one might expect more,
but while the theme persists, so shall I.

Moulth's account of the sylphs (to follow) is clearly akin
to that in the *Comte de Gabalis*, and I have already pointed to the
ready convergence with Albertine works, and also of course the
overarching 'Mythographer' figure of Paracelsus or Pseudo-
Paracelsus. It is hardly important which, as concerns conjure books
involving Elementals, which are apparently a more unified genre
than may have been suspected not long ago in the grimoire world.

In short, Moulth is no more inventing his characters than
Walter Scott invented folklore. He is riffing on a theme – a language
even – other authors and readers clearly know about, and within

which they can and do think, apparently more deeply and eruditely than we had suspected.

The sylphs, inhabitants of the air, are genii or elemental spirits who know and adore God, who love virtuous and chaste men. The Platonists and the Persians acknowledge these kind creatures, intermediaries between man and immaterial creatures. Also, they did not assume them completely free from any material; **but the precise determination of their nature and hierarchy does not go back beyond the Middle Ages when they were discovered by sages to whom the sylphs revealed themselves.** [My emphasis. Clearly the revolution in thought he means is the Paracelsian one].

Formed from the most subtle particles of air, they are invisible to us when they do not have a material body, which they can do at will. They have a soul, but it is not immortal; although living for many centuries, they die without going through the disadvantages and the infirmities of old age. They would live in innocence and perfect happiness, were the idea of death and the complete annihilation of their being not so tormenting. It is for this reason that they seek the attendance of Eve's daughters because this frequentation gives them immortality. The children born of a sylph and a woman, or of a man and a sylph, have a material body like us and an immortal soul like ours; but they are born with a superior intelligence that soon acquires them a sort of domination and power over men. Alexander the Great, the prophet Merlin, and various other great men of antiquity and modern times, existed through such attendance.[11]

---

11 Moulth, *Petit manuel*, pp. 17-18.

Whatever we may feel about marriages between ourselves and elemental spirit species, renouncing human alliances in a manner more monogamous than celibate, more is concerned in these accounts. Paracelsian Elementals do not represent new beings as such, but a new ontology of beings described in other manners elsewhere, such as within religions and mythologies past and present. For our purposes I suggest restricting its use to an analytical tool within relevant 'Western' materials, be they grimoires, folk traditions, or pagan religio-mythic themes as they relate to various magic related topics – a 'thought-tool' for operational purposes, enabling us to enter a coherent and intelligible ritual-and-research paradigm, rather than venturing into what we might term 'beliefs'.

In the case of the two 'great men' mentioned above, this implies that – for example – we can reconsider the old idea that Alexander's 'real' father was not King Philip of Macedon but a god: Ammon in some ancient accounts. Paracelsian mythic ontology accepts the context of the example – a useful ability when trying to think mythically – but defines or discusses it in different terms than its sources, which 'just happen' to define an area of talismanic and conjuring magic in need of ontological tools and terminology. Ammon then, was in fact a major representative of one or other Elemental race (we may reasonably suspect the fiery one), consorting with his mother Olympias. In this way is explained the divine reptilian form associated with the conception story, according with other parts of Olympias' sorcerous reputation. It is also simple, by the way, to conform this narrative with Empedoclean elemental thought, via ancient syncretism of Ammon and Zeus, in Paracelsian terms the King of the Salamanders.

Let us for now depart their fiery realms and return to the cool fresh aerial domains of Paralda and her Sylphide people:

These gracious beings, full of sweetness and kindness, have their own form of government and laws. They obey their queen Paralda, who has her symbolic palace in the star alpha of the constellation Virgo, and whose signature is the fifth upon our table of occult characters, in the bottom line of the board. They cultivate literature, music, and the occult sciences, and have a passionate love of dance and perfumes. It is believed that they have sometimes been seen playing the harp and to dance in the clouds, as told by the scalds or Scandinavian bards, and in Ossian's poems.

Only true adepts can predict the future through communication with the revealing sylphs, which dictate the answers they must write. Here is how we manage to put ourselves in touch with them, according to St. Thomas, Bodin, Del Rio, Paracelsus, Vossius, etc., etc.

We must first be virtuous and our chastity fool proof to any test, which generally makes this evocation very difficult for people. We then make a talisman by the method which we indicate in our special chapter of Talismans, on a metal or alloy of the seven planetary metals. Besides which detail, you act absolutely as we say in the cited chapter.

The magic square is three strips of three boxes each, and its number of 15 as seen here [the square of Saturn, unconnected to the images used].

5	10	3
4	6	8
9	2	7

The other side of the plate, we engrave with the figure of Paralda, that is, a woman sitting on a cloud, having the left hand resting on a wind harp, and holding a star on her extended right hand. [Note how this description does

not match the figure given earlier, which has Venusian and
Lunar characteristics]. Her name, in Sanskrit characters,
is engraved on top of her head; around the circle, which
does not have a polygon, we engrave the sign of the planet
that entered the degree of the zodiac where is Paralda
(alpha Virgo) when we were making the talisman. We also
engrave the Sign[s?] of the zodiac and of the planets that
are in good aspect. You'll understand all this perfectly by
reading our first chapter: 'On Astrology'.

To make the invocation, you go, at a time that is neither
too hot nor too cold, with a pure sky without any clouds, in
the middle of a plain, near a stream, half an hour after the
sun sets. You choose a solitary place, picturesque, where
you cannot hear bells, barking dogs or crowing roosters.
There, you lay on the grass a triangular piece of pale
pink fabric, and you place on it your talisman, so that it
is exposed in the rays of the moon, which is named triple
Hecate when she presides over the enchantments. You take
care also that the star and moon be seen by each other. You
wait until you hear the sylphs play in the foliage of willows
and poplars by the stream, and you will recognize their
presence by a soft, light wind that will shake the leaves a
little, and will gently ride the surface of the clear waters of
the stream Then you will burn, on a small tripod of silver
gilt, the perfumes of the day, that you will have made.

As Cardan, Paracelsus, the two Alberts and a host
of other wise men said, elemental spirits, sylphs, gnomes,
undines and salamanders, love many perfumes; but every
day of the week has its own. If it is, as I suppose, Friday that
you make your evocation, you will take to compose your
perfume, musk, ambergris, aloe wood, dry roses and red
coral [this recipe is from the *Petit Albert*, which has perfumes
for the seven days embedded in a discussion of elementals,

including Gnomes and the *Prayer of the Salamanders* among other commonalities with this text, *Gabalis* etc. See also my *Sworn and Secret Grimoire*]. You pulverize everything, you add blood of turtledove, and the brains of two or three sparrows, to make it a kind of thick paste that you then put in small grains the size of a seed of vetch. You dry for yourself to serve as needed. You light your fire in a small stove earth, new and very clean, with very dry wood of laurel and hazel, which you set on fire by means of a piece of fire making flint which you strike with a piece of steel. Observe that the stone, the wick, the match and the candle which you will use for it are new and have not been used for any secular purpose. Observe also to cast your scent balls in the fire only three by three. When the perfume starts to burn and spread its odour, you will turn your eyes to the star and say three times, aloud:

O Paralda! powerful queen of the air, friend of the Sun, of Hecate and Venus (of Venus if it is Friday, Mars if it is Tuesday, etc.), deign to send to my help one of your faithful servants, in the name of amber and rose.

After this invocation you let the fire go out, you will throw the ashes in the wind, and you will retire to your home. If, while you are on your way, you do not hear the owl's mournful song, nor the slight rustling of the wing of a bat or an owl, if your dog does not bark at the moon when you come home, then go peacefully to bed with the certainty that the night will not end without a [male or female] sylph coming to visit you, and relaying with the greatest kindness answers to all the questions regarding your future, etc., if only in a dream.[12]

---

12 Moulth, *Petit manuel*, pp. 18-22.

PRACTICAL IMPLICATIONS

Be it noted before these considerations that in Albert the Great's
massively influential *Speculum Astronomiae*, astrological talismans are
divided into three classes: the 'abominable', the merely 'detestable'
and the 'permitted'. His example of the most 'abominable' and
'necromantic' astrological talismans concerns a method involving
the Lunar Mansions, suspected strongly of demonic connections.
Many astrological magicians since, including for example Cornelius
Agrippa, anxious to remain within the fold and escape condemnation,
followed his 'permitted' route. My strategy in exploring traditional
magic has been to take the exact opposite tack: the darker the
traditional reputation, the more likely it is to contain grains of an
untampered and effective magic, a rule of thumb which has served
me well. It is likely that Lunar Mansion magic has remained largely
neglected for so long partly through adherence to Albert's line, and
partly through the lack of resources resulting from it.

These cautionary preliminaries having now been conducted,
there are various aspects to Moulth's adaptations of *Petit Albert*
talismans, and the talismanic invocation of Paralda, that may
usefully be discussed or elaborated in context of my own purposes
in writing. These talismans were introduced in amended form in
The Sworn and Secret Grimoire[13] and can serve as our base.

As the polygons Moulth introduces are a little inscrutable
to me and reduce available space, they may be dispensed with,
while his varying the god names used is an excellent start point. If
considering magical alphabets for writing these names, one could
usefully prioritise two potential replacements for Moulth's Sanskrit.
The first is the Alphabet of the Magi, associated with Paracelsian
astrological talismans already. In addition, the so-called Theban

---

13 Jake Stratton-Kent, *The Sworn and Secret Grimoire* (West Yorkshire:
Hadean Press, 2021), pp. 26-38.

script recommends itself to us first by employing the Latin alphabet as its base rather than 'qabalistic Hebrew', and secondly by its resemblance to the Georgian alphabet, evoking connections with Colchis and Medea.

His changing of the image on the Paralda talisman makes it a little unclear whether he is outright identifying Hecate with Paralda, but I shall assume he is not. There are of course valid reasons to use a traditional image of Hecate on lunar talismans rather than his allegorical figure anyway. Such images have been employed upon countless talismans in the past and will assist a segue with rituals from the *PGM* and elsewhere. However, while images of the gods are appropriate, there are equally valid reasons to employ other images altogether. A pictorial image of a 'demon' or elemental associated with the Mansion in question is one example (for example, Leonard with his three horns, or an equivalent image of Lucifuge Rofocale).

ANIMAL FORMS

In the many versions of Lunar Mansion symbols, there is a great preponderance of animal symbols, far more so than the Zodiac, and much closer to the lesser known *dodekuaros* (animal symbols of the hours from Hellenic times). This speaks of greater antiquity, or a closer alignment with less 'civilised' traditions. In my experimental work I have employed this connection in various ways: photos of animals taken in my own environment; Egyptian-style animal headed gods as images; or god-forms (more properly 'therio-forms') as motifs on talismans, and so forth. Thus, the animal forms associated with the Mansions suggest other routes. Physical images of the animals are strongly recommended for the working altar, as are temporary or permanent pictorial 'icons'. In the case of Spica, one might visualise a cat-headed goddess blessing the talisman during the ritual, with such words as 'it is not my hand which consecrates this talisman, it is the hand of N that does this deed' (where N represents the name of the goddess or spirit invoked). With the more 'barbaric' conjurations of the papyri or the *Picatrix*, or original compositions on similar lines, the employment of such techniques is extremely potent, and nudges 'ceremonial magic' in under-explored but equally 'traditional' directions. Other uses will suggest themselves to the keen and resourceful student.

SIGILS

The sigils upon the talismans in *Sworn and Secret Grimoire* will serve us well alongside animal or god images, but here again, there are alternatives depending how one goes about Lunar Mansion work with the materials presented here. Spirit sigils from the *Petit Manuel* itself, or from the *Grimorium Verum* are strong contenders for experiment. Again, this is not exhaustive; the sigils of the Behenian stars from Agrippa should certainly be considered, alongside the animal, plant, and stone correspondences.

OF THE BEHENIAN STARS AND MAGICAL MATERIALS

The nature of gods on earth] doth consist, Asclepius, of plants, and stones, and spices, which contain the nature of [their own] divinity. And for this cause they are delighted with repeated sacrifice, with hymns, and lauds, and sweetest sounds, tuned to the key of Heaven's harmonious song. So that what is of heavenly nature, being drawn down into the images by means of heavenly use and practices, may be enabled to endure with joy the nature of mankind, and sojourn with it for long periods of time.

The Perfect Sermon; or the Asclepius XXXVIII 1 & 2
(in Mead, pp. 383-384)

Work with natural materials like stones, herbs, and images is strikingly absent from the 'popular' conception of Solomonic ritual, due partly to logocentric emphases in modern and not-so-modern society. The same over-emphasis is present at times in Solomonic magic but is by no means a rule. Either way this is a failing which a neo-Paracelsian revolution is particularly suited to address. That theurgists like Iamblichus considered magical work employing 'materia' essential, distinguishing themselves from more conventional philosophers in the process, is an important point. It also underlies the Hermetic theory of 'god making', which the theurgic conception essentially reflects rather than originates. Nevertheless, decan images and the 'correspondences' employed with them is part of the inheritance embodied in the *Testament of Solomon* and is readily applied equally appropriately – if not more so – to the Lunar Mansions. As with the decans, the spirit catalogue and the magical processes of the mansion literature are essentially a unified whole. Acknowledged or not, this work is an aspect of evocation; powerful instances, only half submerged, can be indicated throughout the grimoire literature.

THE BEHENIAN STARS, THEIR SPIRITS, AND MAGICAL COMPONENTS

STAR	MINERAL	PLANT	ANIMAL	VERUM SPIRIT	STAR SIGIL
Algol	Diamond	Black Hellebore, Mugwort		Flerity	
Pleiades	Crystal Quicksilver	Frankincense, Fennel		Flerity	
Aldebaran	Ruby, Carbuncle	Lady's Thistle, Woodruff		Belzebuth	
Capella	Sapphire	Horehound, Mint, Mugwort, Mandrake		Sargatanas	
Sirius	Beryl	Juniper, Mugwort, Dragons Wort	Tongue of a Snake	Astaroth	
Procyon	Agate	Flowers of Marigold, Pennyroyal		Astaroth	
Regulus	Garnet	Sallendine, Mugwort, Mastic		Musisin	

Alkaid	Lodestone	Mugwort, Chicory, Flowers of Periwinkle	Tooth of a wolf	Frimost	
Gienah	Black onyx (and similar)	Henbane, Comfrey, Flowerheads of Burdock, Daffodil.	Tongue of a frog	Klepoth	
Spica	Emerald	Sage, Trifoil, Periwinkle, Mugwort, Mandrake		Khil	
Arcturus	Jasper	Plantain		Khil	
Alphecca	Topaz	Trifoil, Ivy, Rosemary		Clisthert	
Antares	Sardonyx, Amethyst	Long Aristolochia, Saffron		Hiepact	
Vega	Chrysolite	Succory, Fumitory		Frucissiere	
Deneb Algedi	Chalced-ony	Marjoram, Mugwort, Nip, Mandrake		Morail	

There is then the question of how and whether to employ planetary or elemental attributions in our ritual frame, and in composing the talisman. I suggest we take a flexible approach to this rather than expect the spirits to always fit our potent but artificial 'frames'. Occasionally I have employed two distinct planetary codings when working with some of the *GV* spirits, suiting them to the purpose and occasion rather than seeing them as contradictory.

One planetary coding is the days of the week associated with seven *GV* spirits, as already discussed in the introduction to this work. The other example – almost completely different – is as follows, with 'Sunday' for example being the 'Day of Creation' corresponding to the Mansion rather than any particular day of the mundane week. As will be seen, among other features, this corresponds Khil with both Air and the Moon, in the same Mansion as that Paralda is connected with.

AN ATTRIBUTION OF THE VERUM SPIRITS TO THE ELEMENTS AND DAYS

	FIRE	WATER	AIR	EARTH
SUNDAY	Lucifer	Nebiros	Kleppoth	Segal
MONDAY	Satanachia	Astaroth	Khil	Frucissiere
TUESDAY	Agliarept	Syrach/Scirlin	Mersilde	Guland
WEDNESDAY	Tarchimache	Claunech	Clisthert	Surgat
THURSDAY	Flerity	Musisin	Sirchade	Morail
FRIDAY	Belzebuth	Bechaud	Hiepact	Frutimier
SATURDAY	Sargatanas	Frimost	Humots	Huictigaras

Such employment of distinct frames with the same family of spirits is beneficial for several reasons, among which must certainly be included delimiting the spirits which, while developing flexibility in the operator and enabling more ground to be covered, makes it a useful habit. That such apparently simple or artificial frames ring archetypal bells, resonating with much older traditions, does recommend them and pique our interest, but need not make any particular frame 'canonical' at the expense of others.

The option of working with a purely elemental scheme, rather than including the planets, is also worth exploring. Four rulers of the elements from among the ancient gods rather than the astrological 'Olympians' are not difficult to find, and this may assist breaking free from classical ideas to more primal conceptions of those same gods. Empedocles associated Zeus, Hera, Hades, and 'Nesta' (an alias for Persephone) with the elements, though – as with the demon kings in the grimoires – opinion differs as to how this was done. One alternative is to pair the pre-Jovist and archaic Poseidon as ruler of floods as well as the Sea with the chthonic Demeter (depicted as mare-headed). This attribution will work well alongside liturgies involving *Pyramidos*. Hecate/Persephone then rules Air, while either Hades or Hephaestus rules Fire. In my opinion this reading also accords sufficiently well with the Agrippan attribution of Oriens, Amaymon, Paimon, and Egyn, with gender being a secondary matter.

PRACTICE

BEGINNING

Some anecdotal 'suggestions' might be more use than skeletonic rites based on unfamiliar super-structures: start with the animals as a focal point, perhaps with other elements (herbs, metals, and stones) already incorporated, perhaps not.

This is experimental, so loosen up and give yourself some freedom of action. Pictures of appropriate animals might be useful – I've had a photo of a local milk-cow on the altar before now. The idea is to explore complementing verbal and written material with visual imagery: a shift in emphasis. Thus, cows in sacred art began to influence workings with the spirit of that Mansion. Pictorial talismans, improvised from the 'alphabets' according to need, substitute for 'by rote' approaches emphasising existing 'geometrical' pentacle designs that may not include your area of current interest anyway. In one operation with the 'cow' spirit, I employed a sigil of the star or constellation characterising the Mansion painted in green on a scallop shell, with a picture of Hathor stuck in the centre. Such improvised artefacts are traditional, and what's more, effective.

Ramping it up, replace the 'god-forms' of Golden Dawn ritual with 'therio-forms'. Thus, consecrating a talisman might involve seeing the spirit in the form of – again – a cat-headed goddess, a figure in the smoke enveloping the talisman. Or yourself, assuming that form and working the concept 'it is not my hand that does N, but the hand of the spirit N'. With the more barbaric conjurations of the papyri or the *Picatrix*, or original compositions on similar lines, the employment of such techniques is extremely potent, and nudges 'ceremonial magic' in under-explored but equally 'traditional' directions.

Whether wishing to identify with a spirit or to call it, the animal form appropriate is very useful for the magician. As part of a more primal and unrestricted 'alphabet', there is less interference typical of more 'theology specific' and artificial overlays which mask the essence and nature of the spirit, and more room for direct communion and real contact, and less for failure.

There is a strong shamanic and archaic basis for this potency, much of it concerning the animal imagery. The divine animals, as remembered in the 'circle of animals' which is the Zodiac, are older than the manlike gods. Behind all names, systems, and philosophies are the numinous creatures, their reality both immediate and spiritual. We share in this magic the archaic responses of our remotest ancestors, untrammelled by language and other distances.

INTEGRATING TRADITIONAL MATERIALS

Using some astrological math or tabulation to facilitate 'overlapping' the Mansions and decans, the grimoire spirit Frimost connects, for example, with the correspondences of the decan god Amphatham. These, and those of the corresponding Mansion and Fixed Star provide the considerations.

- Decan Image: Osiris, crowned, bandaged and holding a staff.

- Mansion Animal (in place of or in addition to Osiris): He goat. Alkaid – the associated Fixed Star – offers the bull or calf, also among its correspondences is the tooth of a wolf.

- Stone: glasslike, (crystal etc). There is other lore concerning stones and Frimost; 'the first stone you find' is a traditional offering. Alkaid's stone is the lodestone, a stone which finds.

- Herb: Blue Succory or Chicory. Additional, mugwort. Occasionally, as advised by the spirits, add herbs of Belzebuth to those of Frimost.

While Moulth would approve of his inclusion, Osiris here does not represent an identification with Frimost; the image implies a god of the Underworld, appropriate enough to Frimost (see my *Frimost & Klepoth*). The image could be, but need not be engraved on a crystal with vetch underneath and set in a ring as in Hellenic decan magic; the correspondences can inform a 'mojo bag' operation instead, for example, goat horn as an ingredient, a talisman with names suited to a working of Frimost, and a goat or Osiris image amidst them. Blue succory may explain why Frimost asks for chicory coffee in my workings with him; it could however be employed as a herbal ingredient in a Cyprian-style talismanic (mojo) bag. Mugwort would be particularly appropriate as an addition in cases involving dreams or purifications.

For making of larger images in clay or wax, for example adapting various rites in the papyri involving magical statues, similar routes apply. The consecration of wax and earth in the *Key of Solomon* has been recommended before and is well worth examining. Messy hands and finely bound grimoires need keeping apart, but the process is hard to improve on in terms of authenticity.

THE SPIRIT CATALOGUE CONTINUED

To continue our examination of the spirit catalogue in detail, what follows is a comparison of the *Heptameron* names of the main catalogue and those given by Moulth.

MAGICAL ELEMENTS	MOULTH
Fatua or Fressina	Fatua or Pressine*
Melusina	Mélusine
Aldebran	Aldebran
Salvania	Sylvania
Dexgar	Duergar**
Deoinehia	Daoinehie
Pie de ciervo	Pied-de-biche
Robino de los bosques	Robin des bois
Alfheino	Alfheim
Svvart	Swart
Omitted	Vidblain
Hodeken	Hodeken
Omitted	L'invisible***
Follet	Follet
Tomptogobe	Tomtegobb
Grisu	Grisou
Kelpic; Norickar	Kelpic; Norickar
Nicneven	Nicneven

Nika	Nixa
Amadria	Amadria
Omitted	Satan or Nikar****
Oldnick	Oldnick
Dobia	Dobie
Galdrakina ó Striga	Galdrakinna or Striga
Geirada	Geirada
Omitted	Ourisk*****
Omitted	Vardoulacka ******
Annaberge	Annaberge
Puck	Puck

* Pressine is the mother of Melusine in British versions of the legend.
** Duergar is a Scandinavian word for Dwarf, note the fire rather than Earth attribution in the next table.
*** L'invisible is unidentified and may involve an in-joke or simply a lost allusion to a description elsewhere.
**** Nikar is another folklore spirit, in horse form, and associated with the sea in Iceland and the Faroe Islands.
***** Ourisk or Urisk, a Scottish spirit of inland water, eager to make friends but terrifying in appearance, so constantly disappointed.
****** Vardoulacka; refers to the vampire, in Hungary, Serbia, Greece etc.

At an earlier point in the text many of these names appear in a table with elemental attributions and ranks, as follows. Some of the names in this table do not directly reproduce those above and elsewhere, and some use of pseudonyms is apparent, some clarified later, others not. For instance, Antares is elsewhere connected with Belzebuth, but 'Aldebran' [sic] is not identified. There is also apparent duplication, as with Hodeken, Hadeken, and presumably Ghob's Kobold minister and the 'Ondine' also have names, and etc.

In any case, the material deserves inclusion here for various reasons ahead of the real meat of the material.

ELEMENT	RANKS
	RULERS
Fire	Djin – King
Air	Paralda – Queen
Water	Nicka/Nicksa – Queen
Earth	Gob – King
	MINISTERS
Fire	'Aldebran'
Air	Pressine
Water	Hadeken
Earth	'Kobold(s)'
	CHIEFS
Fire	Duergar
Air	Melusine
Water	'Ondine'
Earth	'Pied-de-Biche'
	PRINCES AND PRINCESSES
Fire	Alfheim
Air	Sylvania
Water	Hodeken
Earth	Robin de Bois

FIFTH POWER	
Fire	Swart
Air	Wilzina
Water	Nayas
Earth	Vidblain
GENIES ERRANT	
Fire	Antares
Air	Baalberith
Water	Beelzabetes
Earth	L'invisible

It seems likely that some deliberate subterfuge, and use of variants and 'blinds' may be at play. A light-hearted and bantering tone in the text might encourage us to consider the material frivolous, but as was shown when commenting on the *Heptameron* in *TCM*, there is more going on with this material, despite the mode of transmission and its apparent target audience of an idle 'fairer sex' dabbling in 'occult lite'; regarding which Pope's description of *Le Comte de Gabalis* might encourage us to look deeper than appearances.

This brings me to the central matter, the references to stars corresponding to these spirits, beginning with the main catalogue again, before discussing the superiors. Here simple tabulation for purposes of illustration will not serve, so a preamble is necessary. The stars are not identified by name in most cases; a Greek letter and the constellation to which they belong is given instead. With some minor difficulties these can be identified and their precessed position in today's night sky established (whence collation with Lunar Mansion material from other sources may follow). This I duly performed and noticed two things in the process. First, the listing was not consecutive, in terms of position on the Ecliptic; secondly, a good many of the stars employed are not part of the traditional Arabic and European mansion schema, but are major Chinese and Indian marker stars. Whoever the author of this material was, they had access to some fairly special astrological sources. This is not a terrific surprise as Chinese and Sanskrit characters appear in both works – some in relation to this very same material – and there is no historical difficulty about such access either. However, utilising astronomical data – at all – plainly goes beyond adopting 'curious figures' into a grimoire context.

Consequently, I first reordered the material into consecutive order in terms of position on the Ecliptic, but otherwise much as given. This was a necessary and an obvious step, but while useful as data, the results did not jump off the page at me. However, I had noticed that while Mansion stars were clearly used and emphasised, only stars from Zodiacal constellations were included (the Mansions involve several additional constellations, all absent here). Following the order of spirits listed, my table had some stars at the end attributed to Aries, first of the Signs.

When I moved these to the beginning, everything became much clearer. The first star mentioned, in consecutive order, counting from the first of the Zodiacal Signs, is the same star many Hindu Sidereal astrologers measure their Zodiac from. Once this hidden order is restored, a clearer picture emerges. It is very far from representing a complete system. The focus on the Signs as Constellations rather than the entire mansion system means there are large blank areas. However, the 'occupied areas' are in themselves interesting, and might be tagged as potential hot spots or placements to watch within an ongoing experimental approach. While 'open ended' and more suggestive than spelled out, this material plainly possesses potential for further exploration. It partially parallels the approach recommended already, and with some mental elasticity could readily be further examined and engaged with alongside.

SPIRIT AND STAR CATALOGUES IN ORDER FROM ARIES THROUGH
PISCES

OTHER SPIRITS	STARS	DATA
Puck	Zeta Pisces	Revati 20° 00' Aries
[Vardoulacka]	Alpha Pisces	Al Risha 29° 22' Aries
Melusine	Beta Aries	Sheratan 3° 58' Taurus
Fatua/ Fressina/Pressine	Alpha Aries	Hamal 7° 40' Taurus
'Aldebaran'	Alpha Taurus	9° 47' Gemini
Salvania	Beta Taurus	El Nath 22° 34' Gemini
Duergar	Zeta Taurus	Al Hecka 23° 47' Gemini
Pied-de-biche	Upsilon Gemini	Tejat Posterior 5° 18' Cancer
Deoinehia	Epsilon Gemini	Mebsuta 9° 56' Cancer
Robin of the forests	Beta Cancer	Al Tarf 4° 16' Leo
Swart	Mu Leo	Ras Elased Borealis 21° 26' Leo
[Vidblain]	Epsilon Leo	Al Jabhah 27° 54' Leo
Alfheino/Alfheim	Gamma Leo	Algieba 29° 37' Leo
Hodeken	Epsilon Virgo	Zania 4° 50' Libra
Grisu	Beta Scorpio	Akrab 3° 12' Scorpio
[The Invisible]	Alpha Libra	Zubenelgenubi 15° 05' Scorpio
Follet	Beta Libra	Zubeneschamali 19° 23' Scorpio

Tomptogobe	Gamma Libra	Zuben Elakrab 25° 09' Scorpio
Kelpie	Gamma Scorpio (Sic. Likely Scorpio G, formerly Gamma Telescopium)	27° 55' Sagittarius
Nika/Nixa	Delta Sagittarius	Kaus Medius 4° 35' Capricorn
Amadria	Zeta Sagittarius	Ascella 13° 38' Capricorn
Nicneven	Alpha Sagittarius	Rukbat 16° 38' Capricorn
Satan or Nikar	Alpha Capricorn	Algedi Prima 3° 46' Aquarius Algedi Secundo 3° 51' Aquarius
Dobia/Dobie	Beta Capricorn	Dabih 4° 03' Aquarius
Geirada	Beta Aquarius	Sadalsuud 23° 24' Aquarius
Oldnick	Delta Capricorn	Deneb Algedi 23° 32' Aquarius
Galdakrina, Striga	Alpha Aquarius	Sadalmelik 3° 21' Pisces
[Ourisk]	Delta Aquarius	Skat 8° 52' Pisces
Annaberge	Beta Pisces	Fum Al Samakah 18° 35' Pisces

To conclude, this material, with all its eccentricities, appears to be the source of the names of the Four Elemental Kings and

Queens employed by, but not originating with Eliphas Levi, from whence they made their way into modern occultism, but without any reference to this previous context. The spirits they preside over are obviously Elementals and folkloric figures – who in our default theology are of course 'sublunar' spirits – and simultaneously spirits of the Lunar Mansions. Individual exploration and experimental work with these raw materials from obscure grimoires is strongly encouraged. Such an open-ended and self-reliant work programme is to be preferred over any hand-held step-by-step course or manual.

ANGELS AS ELEMENTAL COHORTS OF THE SCOTT CATALOGUE

Moulth's introducing angels of the elements, ruled by Scott's folkloric spirits, may seem anachronistic, but is in fact an example of his Paracelsian iconoclasm, and there is also much more to the matter than appears. Note carefully for instance that although in 'generic' occultism Shemhamforash 'angels' are frequently encountered associated with the decans, Moulth's attribution clearly connects them with the Lunar Mansions instead. Before we proceed though, in the first place let us examine again the claim of the *Grimorium Verum* (p. 50):

> In the first part is taught the means of calling forth the Elemental Spirits of the Air, Earth, Sea and Infernus, according to the correct correspondences.

Here, notably, we see Fire as a subterranean power, rather than an empyrean one. This arrangement places the so-called salamanders in an underworld context, in closer proximity to the earthy gnomes than the starry heavens, a conception encountered elsewhere in Cyprianic and other grimoires. We should recall too that Hephaestus or Vulcan, the god of fire, represents both volcanos and flammable underground gas emissions (such fiery hills as resulted probably precede the volcanic connection). So too, indisputably, the 'demons' of the grimoire are here seen as elemental spirits. Turning from the goetic to the 'neo-theurgic' view of Cornelius Agrippa (TBOP III xvi, p. 500), we find angels no less interwoven with animistic conceptions of the elemental kingdoms, and simultaneously overlapping with folkloric spirits:

Whence as these angels are appointed for divers stars, so also [others] for divers places and times, not that they are limited by time or place, neither by the bodies which they are appointed to govern, but because the order of wisdom hath so decreed; therefore they favour more, and patronise those bodies, places, times, stars; so they have called some diurnal, some nocturnal, other meridional; in like manner some are called woodmen, some mountaineers, some fieldmen, some domestics.

Hence the gods of the woods, country gods, satyrs, familiars, fairies of the fountains, fairies of the woods, nymphs of the sea, the Naiades, Neriades, Dryades, Pierides, Hamadryades, Potumides, Hinnides, Agapte, Pales, Pareades, Dodonæ, Feniliæ, Lavernæ, Pareæ, Muses, Aonides, Castalides, Heliconides, Pegasides, Meonides, Phebiades, Camenæ, the Graces, the Genii, hobgoblins, and such like; whence they call them vulgar superiors, some the demigods and goddesses.

Some of these are so familiar and acquainted with men, that they are even affected with humane perturbations, by whose instruction *Plato* thinketh that men do oftentimes wonderful things.

Here plainly 'angels' as a category is elastic enough to comprehend both hobgoblins and the lower pagan deities. Thus, Moulth's folkloric spirits reigning over equally elemental angels is not so peculiar, occult lore some centuries previous being equally flexible. The approximate contemporaneity of Agrippa, Paracelsus, and Moulth's cabalist, Palingene, is also apropos. That there was a sea change in grimoire magic of which Paracelsus was a pivot is well expressed by Sir Walter Scott:

> ...because the earlier astrologers, though denying the use of all necromancy, that is, unlawful or black magic, pretended always to a correspondence with the various spirits of the elements, on the principles of the Rosicrucian philosophy. They affirmed they could bind to their service, and imprison in a ring, a mirror, or a stone, some fairy, sylph, or salamander, and compel it to appear when called, and render answers to such questions as the viewer should propose.[14]

This sounds suspiciously akin to a Paracelsian rewriting of otherwise familiar goetic grimoire and practical hermetic themes, Elementals instead of – or masking – grimoire spirits, who, reaccommodated in elemental guise, were enclosed in rings and mirrors as before. While subterfuge may be suggested here, what it really represents is an alternative analytic ontology for viewing spirits of every period, folk culture, and religion, and an escape from strictly biblical takes.

So, too, in the *Compendious Apology for the Society called Rosicrucian* written by Robert Fludd, it is stated that the Seraphim, Virtues, and Powers are of a fiery character, the Cherubim are terrestrial, the

---

14 Walter Scott, *Letters*, p. 339.

Thrones and Archangels are aquatic, while the Dominations and Principalities are aerial'.[15] As already observed, angels could long be viewed as sublunar and 'elemental', even if these characteristics were elsewhere also attributed to demons. Here it is taken a step further, and 'angels' are taken as counterparts of the inferiors of chiefs who are undoubtedly folkloric spirits and Elemental rulers.

TABLE OF THE ELEMENTAL GENII ACCORDING TO THE CABALIST
PALINGENE*

ELEMENT	RANKS	COHORTS	COHORTS	COHORTS
	RULERS			
Fire	Djin – King	Vehuiah	Silael [Sitael]	Mahasiah
Air	Paralda – Queen	Leuviah	Nelchael	Melahel
Water	Nicka/Nicksa – Queen	Aniel	Rehahel	Bahabel
Earth	Gob – King	Mebahia	Nemamiah	Harabel
	MINISTERS			
Fire	'Aldebran'	Achaiah	Hazel	Laviah
Air	Pressine	Nethhaiah	Jerathel	Reyel
Water	Hadeken	Vevaliah	Scaliah	Azaliah
Earth	'Kobold'	Umabel	Annavel	Damabiah
	CHIEFS			
Fire	Duergar	Jesalel	Hariel	Leviah

15 A. E. Waite, *The Occult Sciences: A Compendium of Transcendental Doctrine and Experiment* (London: Kegan Paul, 1891) p. 37.

Air	Melusine	Lecabel	Jehuiah	Chavakiah
Water	'Ondine'	Vehuel	Hahasiah	Nanael
Earth	'Pied-de-Biche'	Ejael	Rochel	Hejajel

PRINCES AND PRINCESSES				
Fire	Alfheim	Jelael [Ieliel]	Elemiah	Lelahel
Air	Sylvania	Pahaliah	Jeiajel	Hahiviah
Water	Hodeken	Haamiah	Jejazel	Michael
Earth	Robin de Bois	Pojel	Jejalel	Mizrael

FIFTH POWER				
Fire	Swart	Caheththel	Aladia	Hahajah
Air	Wilzina	Haaiah	Sechiah	Omael
Water	Nayas	Jelahiah	Ariel	Mismael
Earth	Vidblain	Jahhel	Mehiel	Manakel

GENIES ERRANT				
Fire	Antares	Mehahel	Hakamiah	Caliel
Air	Baalberith	Vasaviah	Leahiah	Manadel
Water	Beelzabetes	Daniael	Imamiah	Nitael
Earth	L'invisible	Habujah	Jabaniah	Mumiah

I have attached to this table, which was drafted by the Cabalist Palingene*, the names of the kings, queens, ministers, princes and princesses, Chiefs and powers engineering. If Palingene left them out, it is because, although a learned magician-Cabalist, he was much less well versed in astrology, which is the Queen of the occult sciences, and maybe could not discover their Palaces in the stars of the constellations. He will not have recognised them for Geniuses and will have confused them with demons and evil spirits, which is a heresy of the occult. In fact, I think Palingène never communicated directly with the sylphs, as everyone knows they are beings very mysterious and very discrete.[16]

*Marcellus Palingenius, aka Pier Angelo Manzolli, the author of the book *Zodiacus Vitae* (Basel, 1543) is believed to be the Neapolitan poet Marcello Stellato, in Latin Marcellus Palingenius Stellatus (born ca. 1500 – died in Cezana before 1551). The Latin poem – in twelve volumes, one for each Zodiacal Sign – distributes the names of the angels of the Shemhamphorash in a manner differing from the familiar format. His work was influential on various French occult authors preceding Levi, as well as Shakespeare, Milton, and others. Moulth's attribution makes folkloric Elementals the superiors and Shemhamforash angels in Palingene's order as their subordinates or 'cohorts'.

Note also how Moulth's concluding remarks assume a clear separation between older magical models and the Paracelsian revolution. While a little triumphalist in tone, such taking of the Paracelsian revolution as a given is a not uncommon feature of the later grimoires, be they Cyprianic, Paracelsian, or Albertine.

Incidentally, regarding the amorphous distinction between rulers and subordinates, demons, and angels, I commend an alternative arrangement on the same theme to the reader's attention.

---

16 Moulth, *Petit manuel*, p. 130.

MANSIONS, SUPERIOR DEMONS, AND COHORTS

LUNAR MANSION CUSPS	VERUM SPIRITS	MANSION ANGELS (FROM AGRIPPA ET AL)
0 Aries	Lucifer	Geniel
12 Aries	Satanachia	Enediel
25 Aries	Agliarept	Amixiel
8 Taurus	Tarchimache	Azariel
21 Taurus	Fleruty	Gabiel
4 Gemini	Belzebuth	Dirachiel
17 Gemini	Sargatanas	Scheliel
0 Cancer	Nebiros	Amnediel
12 Cancer	Astaroth	Barbiel
25 Cancer	Scirlin	Ardesiel
8 Leo	Claunech	Neciel
21 Leo	Musisin	Abdizuel
4 Virgo	Bechaud	Jazeriel
17 Virgo	Frimost	Ergediel
0 Libra	Klepoth	Ataliel
12 Libra	Khil	Azeruel
25 Libra	Mersilde	Adriel
8 Scorpio	Clisthert	Egibiel
21 Scorpio	Sirchade	Amutiel
4 Sagittarius	Hiepact	Kyriel
17 Sagittarius	Humots	Bethnael
0 Capricorn	Segal	Geliel
12 Capricorn	Frucissiere	Requiel

25 Capricorn	Guland	Abrinael
8 Aquarius	Surgat	Aziel
21 Aquarius	Morail	Tagriel
4 Pisces	Frutimier	Alheniel
17 Pisces	Huictigaras	Amnixiel

NOTES ON THE SUBORDINATE SPIRITS

Turning now to the spirits named in Palingene's table, there is a truly immense fund of folklore material contained and alluded to in the corresponding section of *TCM*. As made apparent therein, this material exemplifies in great detail the type of spirits described in sources like the *Fourth Book* as distinct from those in explicitly demonic catalogues.

There is another kinde of Spirits, which we have spoken of in our third book of Occult Philosophy, not so hurtful, and nearest unto men; so also, that they are effected with humane passions, and do joy in the conversation of men, and freely do inhabit with them: and others do dwell in the Woods and Desarts: & others delight in the company of divers domestique Animals and wilde Beasts; and othersome do inhabit about Fountains and Meadows. Whosoever therefore would call up these kinde of Spirits, in the place where they abide, it ought to be done with odoriferous perfumes, and with sweet sounds and instruments of Musick, specially composed for the business, with using of Songs, Inchantments and pleasant Verses, with praises and promises.

But those which are obstinate to yield to these things, are to be compelled with Threatnings, Comminations, Cursings, Delusions, Contumelies, and especially by threatening to expel them from those places where they are conversant.

Further, if need be, thou maist betake thee to use Exorcismes; but the chiefest thing that ought to be observed, is, constancy of minde, and boldness, free, and alienated from fear.

Lastly, when you would invocate these kinde of Spirits, you ought to prepare a Table in the place of invocation, covered with clean linen; whereupon you shall set new bread, and running water or milk in new earthen vessels, and new knives. And you shall make a fire, whereupon a perfume shall be made. But let the Invocant go unto the head of the Table, and round about it let there be seats placed for the Spirits, as you please; and the Spirits being called, you shall invite them to drink and eat. But if perchance you shall fear any evil Spirit, then draw a Circle about it, and let that part of the Table at which the Invocant sits, be within the Circle, and the rest of the Table without the Circle.[17]

So too these spirits are clearly identical to those folkloric entities in the appendix to Reginald Scot's *Discoverie of Witchcraft*, which with the above I have cited before, but there is ample corroboration elsewhere. There is, in short, no question they are appropriate figures for grimoire magicians to work with. The folkloric background to Moulth's spirit catalogue was explored in *TCM*, albeit based on an incomplete source. Some improvements

---

17 Heinrich Cornelius Agrippa (attrib.), *The Fourth Book of Occult Philosophy* (London: Askin Publishers, 1978) pp. 68-69.

result from Moulth's rendering of a few spellings, which were misleading in the *Heptameron* variant. These amendments and some additional references to a few other spirits are detailed below, for the larger portion of the catalogue the account in *TCM* will suffice.

The very first figure in the spirit catalogue has two names, one of which is Pressine, a fairy queen who was the mother of Melusine, the next figure in the series. Her other name is Fatua, a variant on Fauna, a Roman goddess of forests and other rural locations such as fields and plains. Elsewhere in the *Petit Manuel* her other name is specifically mentioned in a catalogue of the Sibyls. The Sibylline tradition is an important topic both in my own previous writings and within the more submerged and previously unacknowledged parts of the grimoire tradition, long prior to Moulth. Given Fatua's first place in the catalogue – a position frequently representing leadership in demonic catalogues and lists of decan gods alike – and the importance of Sibyls, I supply this account of them from a near contemporary of our text:

SIBYLS

The existence of Sibyls dates back to the most haunting antiquity; the Greeks gave this name to all women they believed inspired by a prophetic spirit. Bekker [Balthasar Bekker, 1634–1698, clerical author, well-meaning 'rationalist' and a key figure in ending the witch hunts in Early Modern times, whose mechanistic explanation of oracles can safely be disregarded] thinks, with more reason, that they were women more fully informed that others, who served as priestesses: Varro, Saint Augustine, Lactance [Lactantius], etc., counted ten: the Sibyls of Persia, Cumae, Libya, Hellespont, Delphi, Samos, Phrygia, Eritrea and of Tibur.

Some authors have added the following:

The Colophon Sibyl, also called Lampusia; she was the daughter of Calchas.
The Sibyl Cassandre [Cassandra], daughter of king Priam, whose true predictions of many destinies to befall, no-one believed.
The Epirote sibyl.
The Thessalian sibyl, named Manto.
The sibyl Carmenta [a Roman goddess of childbirth] mother of King Evanta.
Fauna, wife and sister of Faunus, King of Italy [Faunus and Fauna are male and female Roman deities of forests and other rural places].

There were still others, but they were much less reputable than the first ten. There are, however, two authors who have maintained that there were only three sibyls: those of Cumae, Delphi and Eritrea.

(1) There are even some who have admitted only one, She is the one who, in supposed Sibylline verses, calls herself a daughter-in-law of Noah.
(2) She was named by Euripides in the prelude to her tragedy, which is entitled *Lamia*. (3) She took her name from her stay in Cumae in Italy: She is the one of which Naevius [probably Quintus Naevius Cordus Sutorius Macro, 21BC –38AD, a prefect of the Praetorian Guard], Pison [Gaius Calpurnius Piso, a senator in the time of Nero], Virgil, etc., spoke. The latter represents her as a madwoman who wrote her verses on leaves of trees that were prey to the winds.
(4) She is the one who predicts the taking of Troy.

(5) Originating from Cumae in the Aeolid, She is also called Amalthea, Demophile, or Herophile.
(6) She was born during the Trojan campaign, She prophesied of the time of Solon and Cyrus.
(7) She returned her answers to Ancyre [probably modern Ankara is meant].
(8) She had her altars and a cult at Tivoli [formerly Tibur]. She it was who, according to Saint Augustine, prophesied in the time of Romulus.

It was the sibyl of Cumae, in Aolid [Aulus Gellius, citing Dionysus of Halicarnussus], that brought to Tarquin the Elder the nine books of Sibylline oracles, she demanded a price so high that the king thought she was mad. Sibylle threw three in the fire and asked for the same price from the other six; Tarquin having refused, she burned three more and still demanded the same price from the remaining three. The surprised king consulted the augurs, who advised him to buy the three books at the required price. He immediately appointed two patricians to keep these precious books, which were consulted in great calamities and by decree of the senate. This superstition would have been excusable if it had not sometimes been accompanied by a sacrifice of human victims.[18]

Returning to the spirit catalogue and corrections to the *Heptameron* focused account in *TCM*, in the case of the fifth spirit, the *Heptameron* gives Dexgar, possibly via the Catalan or Portuguese: 'deixar' or abandoned, which misled me at the time of writing. Moulth gives the proper orthography from Scott. Duergar is a

---

18 Julia Fontenelle, Jean Sebastian Eugène, M. Comte, *Nouveau manuel complet des sorciers ou la magie blanche* (Paris: Roret, 1837), p. 53-55.

Scandinavian word for Dwarf, workers with fire and metal, like their diminutive cousins the Dactyls, renowned founders of the goetic mysteries. I extract the following elucidation from another, lesser, French 'manuel', *Nouveau manuel complet des sorciers ou la magie blanche*:

> The ancient chronicles of almost all peoples, especially those of the north, relate the marvellous tales of a class of dwarves, mountain dwellers who are constantly busy forging enchanted weapons. They can be viewed as the species of *gnomes* known as the *duergar*, which are almost always invisible... and who should be kept from being outraged by improper words. The mountaineers never speak of it without the greatest respect.
>
> The Scots born dwarves are even more formidable. They are capricious and cruel. They preferably inhabit conical hills. Circular marks on the ground make known the places where they dance during the night.[19]

Similarly, where Cyprian's *Heptameron* has Deoinehia (spirit 6) Moulth gives Daoinehie, which also enables a better analysis than in *TCM*: the derivation of the name from Scott can be safely relied upon. This is derived from (Irish) Daoine Sidhe or (Scottish) Daoine Sith, the people of the mounds, a term familiar in Irish and Scottish Gaelic and folklore studies.

Hodeken (Spirit 11) is referred to at length by Reginald Scot (*Discoverie*, p. 438) who calls him Hudgin, and 'a very familiar devil'. In the marginal notes he elucidates further:

> Hudgin of Germany, and Rush of England. which will do no body hurt, except he receive injury: but he cannot abide that, nor yet be mocked: he talketh with men friendly,

---

19 Fontenelle, et. al, *Nouveau manuel complet des sorcierse*, p. 75.

sometimes visibly, and sometimes invisibly. There go as many tales upon this Hudgin, in some parts of Germany, as there did in England of Robin Good-fellow. But this Hudgin was so called, because he alwayes wore a Cap or a Hood; and therefore I think it was Robin Hood. Fryer Rush was for all the world such another fellow as this Hudgin, and brought up even in the same School; to wit, in a Kitchin; in so much as the self same tale is written of the one as of the other, concerning the Skullion, which is said to have been slain, &c. for the reading whereof I referr you to Fryer Rush his story, or else to John Wierus: (J. Wier. lib. de praest. daem. 1. cap. 23. De Praestigiis Daemonum).

The above passage is referenced by Walter Scott in his *Letters*, So too Reginald Scot (*Discoverie*, p. 518) gives further detail and agreement regarding Master Hoemmerling (23), who Moulth also refers to as Annaberge in his various tables:

An Example of a turbulent Spirit. Such was Anaebergius a most virulent Animal that did utterly confound the undertakings of those that laboured in the richest Silver mine in Germany, called Corona Rosacea. He would often shew himself in the likeness of a he-goat with Golden horns, pushing down the workmen with great violence, sometimes like a Horse breathing flames, and pestilence at his Nostrils. At other times he represented a Monk in all his Pontificalilus, flouting at their Labour, and imitating their Actions with scorn and dedignation, till by his daily and continued molestation he gave them no further ability of perseverance.

As already seen, Moulth's chief inspiration, Walter Scott, was as capable as I am of citing Reginald Scot, and does so concerning our 24th spirit, Puck (*Letters*, p. 149):

It would require a better demonologist than I am to explain the various obsolete superstitions which Reginald Scot has introduced as articles of the old English faith, into the preceding passage. I might indeed say the Phuca is a Celtic superstition, from which the word Pook or Puckle was doubtless derived; and I might conjecture that the man-in-the-oak was the same with the Erl-König of the Germans; and that the hellwain were a kind of wandering spirits, the descendants of a champion named Hellequin, who are introduced into the romance of Richard sans Peur.

That Reginald Scot influenced Moulth's main inspiration, Sir Walter Scott, may be read poetically as connecting said English author – a main source for the spirit catalogue of the Solomonic *Goetia* – with Moulth, our current demonologist and composer of another spirit catalogue which, we may be assured, is linked inextricably to the Lunar Mansions, to which subject we now return.

THE LUNAR MANSIONS CONTINUED

SAMPLE FIXED STAR POSITIONS AND OTHER FEATURES OF THE MANSIONS

HEAVEN OF SUMMER OR ORMUZD

1: Equinoctial point, 0 Aries.

DENEB KAITOS, 2° 35' Aries. Beta Ceti, a Saturnian star according to Ebertin.

ALGENIB, 9° 09' Aries. Alpha Pegasi; Pegasus has a long history as a Mansion constellation. Mars/Mercury nature (Ebertin).

2: SIRRAH AKA ALPHERATZ, 14° 18' Aries. Alpha Andromeda. Venus/ Jupiter.

3: MIRACH, 00° 24' Taurus. Beta Andomedae, the Navel of

Andromeda, fortunate in honours and matrimony. Of the nature of Venus and Mercury (Agrippa), some say Jupiter/Saturn, and Venus/Neptune (Ebertin). Agrippa mentions it before listing the 15 Behenian stars and their planetary associations. Mirach is not considered one of them, but the constellation has long been associated with the Mansions.

MESARTHIM, 3° 11' Taurus. Gamma Arietis, a traditional Mansion star, once the closest star in Aries to the Vernal Equinoctial point. Ruled by Venus.

SHARATAIN, 3° 58' Taurus. Beta Arietis, Mars/Saturn, a traditional Mansion star.

HAMAL, 7° 40' Taurus. Alpha Aries, 'The Rams Eye' of Agrippa etc: Unlucky, violence, danger, cruelty, head injury. Suffering in love, perversion. Mars/Saturn.

4: ALAMAK, 14° 14' Taurus. Gamma Andromeda, Venus with faint Jupiter-like influence (Ebertin).

5: CAPUT ALGOL, 26° 10' Taurus. Malefic. Decapitation, Fires, sickness, violence, murder. Good success to petitions, maketh a man bold and magnanimous, preserveth the members of the body sound: helpeth against witchcraft, reflecteth evil endeavours and wicked incantations upon our adversaries (Agrippa). Its stone is the Diamond, its plant black hellebore and mugwort. Behenian star, with sigil and data in Agrippa. Saturn/Jupiter.

MEROPE, 29° 42' Taurus (Pleiades).

STEROPE, (i), 29° 44' Taurus (Pleiades).

ALCYONE, 00° 00' Gemini (Pleiades). Crying, unlucky, exile, suffering.

ATLAS, 00° 21' Gemini (Pleiades).

PLEIONE, 00° 23' Gemini (Pleiades).

Operations of the Pleiades: To increase the light of the eyes, assemble spirits. raise winds, reveal secret and hidden things. The stone is crystal, plants frankincense and fennel, metal quicksilver. Behenian star, with sigil and data in Agrippa.

6: ALDEBARAN, 9° 47' Gemini. A Royal Star: courage, war-mongering, military leadership, danger of violence or sickness. Riches and honour. carbuncle, ruby, lady's thistle and woodruff. Behenian star, with sigil and data in Agrippa.

RIGEL, 16° 50'. Beta Orion, Gemini. Success in technical arts, artistic ability, inventive, ambition, lucky.

7: CAPELLA, 21° 51' Gemini (Auriga). Favour of princes. Behenian star, with sigil and data in Agrippa who calls it the Goat Star. Stone: sapphire – plant horehound, mint, mugwort and mandrake.

BELLATRIX, Gamma Orion, 20° 57 Gemini. Accidents, sudden dishonour, fond of power, talkative, trouble through love affairs, jealousy, unlucky.

ALNILAM, buckle of Orions belt – Epsilon Orion, 23° 28' Gemini. Brief fame, quick temper, scandal, good for military, sports, law, church, science. Headstrong. Studious. Possible violent death. The stars of the belt are often called the Three Kings.

POLARIS, Alpha Ursa Minor, 28° 34' Gemini.

BETELGEUSE, Alpha Orion, 28° 45' Gemini. Good fortune, success, fame, shrewd, rash, changeable, inventive, determined, a rebel, fevers, acute illness.

8: Solsticial point 0° Cancer.

ALHENA, 9° 06' Cancer. Gamma Geminorum, Venus with Jupiter influence.

9: SIRIUS, 14° 05' Cancer (Greater Dog Star). Luck, pride, wealth, ambition, good reputation, fame, honours, occult interests, dog bites. Honour and good will, the favour of men and of aerial spirits, giveth power to pacify and reconcile kings, princes and other men. Stone: beryl – Plant: savin, mugwort and dragonwort, (and among animals the tongue of a snake). Behenian star, with sigil and data in Agrippa.

CASTOR, 20° 14' Cancer. Alpha Geminorum. Mercury with Jupiter.

POLLUX, 23° 13' Cancer. Beta Geminorum. Strong Mars influence; can be brutal, tyrannical and cruel.

PROCYON, 25° 47' Cancer (Lesser Dog Star). Conferreth the favour of the gods, spirits and men; protects from evil magics and preserveth health. Stone: achates, plants the flowers of marigold, and pennyroyal. Behenian star, with sigil and data in Agrippa.

10: PRAESEPE, 7° 20' Leo. The Beehive Cluster, traditionally The Manger. Wider orbs to conjunctions than usual with Fixed Stars due to the two Aselli flanking it. Moon/Mars, Ebertin adds with Neptune influence. It is highly unusual to find a Lunar attribution to a Fixed Star, correspondences are usually planetary only. Malefic, bad for eyesight; infectious disease and addiction. Chinese astrology associates it with ancestors and with a lunar conjunction it grants strange experiences involving the world of the dead, or mediumship. A necromancer's star, to be handled with care.

11: KOCHAB, 13° 20' Leo. Beta Ursa Minoris. Saturn/Venus. Little studied.

SERTAN or ACCUBENS, 13° 39' Leo. Alpha Cancri. Mars/Saturn. A sinister star, conducive to deceit and mental instability.

12: ALPHARD, 27° 17' Leo. Alpha Hydrae, Saturn nature, with a measure of influence from Venus and Neptune (Ebertin). Unfortunate: poisons, poisonous bites and suffocation, etc.

REGULUS, 29° 50' Leo. Alpha Leo. Cor Leonis. Glory, wealth, and great honours, chiefly by military preferment, makes a man temperate, appeaseth wrath and giveth favour. Stone: garnet (not, I believe, granite as usually given) – plants: sallendine, mugwort and mastic. Behenian star, with sigil and data in Agrippa.

13: MIZAR, 15° 42' Virgo. Tail of the Great Bear, of the nature of Mars, and conducive to conflagrations and massacres.

14: ALKAID (Benetnash). 26° 56' Virgo. Tail of Ursa Major:. 'Availeth against incantations, and maketh a man secure in his travels'. It is worth noting that the full name of this star in Arabic refers to female professional mourners of the type associated with the origins of goetia (see Geosophia etc). It is counted a malefic star. Its stone is the lodestone and plants succory, mugwort, flowers of periwinkle, and among animals the tooth of a wolf. Behenian star, with sigil and data in Agrippa.

HEAVEN OF WINTER OR AHRIMANES

15: Equinoctial point, 0 Libra.

GIENAH's old unprecessed position (7 Libra) is sometimes reckoned a malefic degree in its own right; the precessed position nevertheless is 10° 44' Libra. Courage, 'naughty dreams', can expel evil spirits or gather them together, good against the malice of men, devils, and winds. Stones such as are of the colour of black onyx stone. Plant: henbane and comfrey, amongst animals the tongue of a frog. Behenian star, with sigil and data in Agrippa who calls it the Wing of the Crow. Of the nature of Saturn/Mars.

16: 13° 27' degrees precessed ALKORAB: a Mansion star mentioned in Agrippa. Of the nature of Saturn/Mars. Strengthens the restraining and limiting nature of Saturn.

SPICA, 23° 50' Libra. Alpha Virginis. Wealth, fame, honour, victory. Sacred to Ishtar the Virgin. Emerald, sage, trifoil, periwinkle, mugwort, mandrake. Behenian star, with sigil, etc. in Agrippa.

ARCTURUS, 24° 14', Libra. Alpha Bootis. Success through patient labour. Jasper, plantain, cf Agrippa who calls it Alcameth. Storms upon the Earth, but riches and honour to those born under it.

17: IZAR, 28° 06' Libra. Epsilon Bootis. Pulcherrima, the Loveliest. Mercury/Saturn. Much odd modern speculation, little astrological use currently, but Bootes is an important magical constellation.

18: ALPHECCA or ELEPHEIA, 12° 18' Scorpio. Alpha Coronae Borealis. Venus/Mercury nature Behenian star with relevant lore in Agrippa.

19: UNUKALHAI ALPHA SERPENTIS, 22° 04' Scorpio. Saturn/Mars nature. Suicide, insanity, accidents, chronic disease. Success in war, politics, writing. Problems in love, shipwreck.

TOLIMAN or BUNGULA, Alpha Centauri. 29° 29' Scorpio. Friends and honour, possible problems relating to women, fatalism.

20: ANTARES, 09° 46' Sagittarius. Alpha Scorpius, Cor Scorpionis. Mars/Jupiter influence. Sardonyx and amethyst, long aristolochia and saffron. see Agrippa et al.

ALWAID, 11° 58' Sagittarius. Beta Draconis, Rastaban. Saturn/Mars.

ALPHA HERCULES, 16° 09' Sagittarius. Ras Algethi. Head of the kneeling Hercules. Mars/Venus with a slight influence from Mercury. Problems or popularity with women, drive for power, courage, boldness, power, fame.

21: RAS ALHAQUE, 22° 27' Sagittarius. Head of Opiuchus. Saturn with some undesirable Venus influences too (Ebertin).

22: Solsticial point, 0 Capricorn.
SPICULUM, the spear, 1° 04' Capricorn. Moon/Mars (Ptolemy). One of many Fixed Stars associated with blindness, and of ill omen.

23: VEGA, 15° 19' Capricorn. Alpha Lyrae. Venus/Mercury. Giveth power over devils and beasts. Chrysolite, succory, and fumitory. See Agrippa who calls it the Falling Vulture.

24: ALTAIR, 1° 47' Aquarius. Alpha Aquila. Mars/Jupiter. Success, boldness, courage, possible bloodshed, and danger from reptiles.

25: DENEB ALGEDI, 23° 33' Aquarius. Delta Capricorni. Saturn/ Jupiter. Bestoweth prosperity and increaseth wrath. Chalcedony. marjoram, mugwort, nip and mandrake root. See Agrippa who calls it Tail of the Goat.

26: FOMALHAUT, 3° 52' Pisces. Alpha Piscis Austrinus. A very famous star, the only one of the four so called 'Persian Royal' stars not among the Behenians. It falls very close to the cusp of the next Mansion, which arguably places it there (an argument for unequal Mansions is beyond the scope of this treatise). It is predominantly but not wholly good, depending on aspects, etc. Its nature is variously given, i.e.: Ptolemy gives Mercury/Venus, Ebertin adds 'with a blending of Neptune influence'.

27: DENEB AGIDE, 5° 20' Pisces. Alpha Cygni. Mercury/Venus influence.

28: SCHEAT, 23° 28' Pisces. Beta Pegasus. Agrippa calls it shoulder of the horse, also called Menkib, again, it is not a Behenian but nevertheless an important Mansion star.

SAMPLE FIXED STAR POSITIONS AND OTHER FEATURES OF THE
MANSIONS

MANSION	ZODIAC DEGREE	STAR NAME OR OTHER	ORB
1st	0° Aries	Equinoctial point.	
1st	2° 35' Aries	Deneb Kaitos. Beta Ceti.	2° 10'
1st	9° 09' Aries	Algenib. Alpha Pegasi.	2° 00'
2nd	14° 18' Aries	Sirrah aka Alpheratz. Alpha Andromeda.	2° 10'
3rd	00° 24' Taurus	Mirach. Beta Andomedae. Navel of Andromeda.	2° 10'
3rd	3° 11' Taurus	Mesarthim.	2° 00'
3rd	3° 58' Taurus	Sharatain. Beta Arietis.	2° 00'
3rd	7° 40' Taurus	Hamal. Alpha Aries, 'The Rams Eye' (Agrippa).	2° 10'
4th	14° 14' Taurus	Alamak. Gamma. Andromeda.	1° 30'
5th	26° 10' Taurus	Caput Algol.	2° 00'

INFLUENCE	NOTES
Saturn (Ebertin)	Inhibitions and restraint.
Mars/Mercury (Ebertin)	Pegasus has a long history as a Mansion constellation. Insight, will and determination, oratory.
Venus/Jupiter	Popularity with Moon, Asc or MC, or the reverse with Sun or Saturn contacts.
Venus/Mercury (Agrippa) Venus/Neptune (Ebertin)	Fortunate in honours and matrimony. Long association with the Mansions. Some give its influence as Jupiter/Saturn; enduring and benign.
Venus (Robson)	A traditional Mansion star. Causes discords and journeys.
Mars/Saturn	A traditional Mansion star. Violent, daredevils and risk, dangers through impetuosity.
Mars/Saturn	Unlucky, violence, danger, cruelty, head injury. Suffering in love, perversion.
Venus with faint Jupiter influence (Ebertin)	Cheerfulness and popularity, diversions and amusements.
Saturn/Jupiter (Agrippa)	Malefic. Decapitation, Fires, sickness, violence, murder. Success to petitions, makes bold and magnanimous, preserves the members of the body sound. Reflects malign upon enemies. Behenian star.

5th	29° 42' 29° 44' 29° 59' Taurus 0° 21' 0° 23' Gemini	Pleiades: Merope Sterope/Asterope Alcyone Atlas Pleione	2° 00'
6th	9° 47' Gemini	Aldebaran. Alpha Tauri.	2° 30'
6th	16° 50' Gemini	Rigel, Beta Orion.	2° 40'
7th	20° 57' Gemini	Bellatrix. Gamma Orionis.	2° 20'
7th	21° 51' Gemini	Capella. Alpha Aurigae. The Goat Star.	2° 40'
7th	23° 28' Gemini	Alnilam, buckle of Orions belt. Epsilon Orionis.	2° 20'
7th	28° 34' Gemini	Polaris. Alpha Ursa Minor.	2° 10'
7th	28° 45' Gemini	Betelgeuse. Alpha Orion.	2° 40'
8th	0° Cancer.	Solsticial point.	
8th	9° 06'Cancer	Alhena. Gamma Geminorum.	2° 20'

	To increase the light of the eyes, assemble spirits. raise winds, reveal secret and hidden things. The Pleiades are traditional Mansion stars and also Behenian, see also the *Testament of Solomon*, etc.
Mars (Agrippa, Ebertin)	A Royal Star: courage, warmongering, military leadership, danger of violence or sickness. Riches and honour. Behenian.
Jupiter/Saturn	Success in technical arts, artistic ability, inventive, ambition, lucky.
Mars/Mercury	Accidents, sudden dishonour, fond of power, talkative, trouble through love affairs, jealousy, unlucky.
Mars/Mercury	'Favour of princes'. Behenian star.
Jupiter/Saturn ('fleeting honours' fits the benign Jupiter, restricted by Saturn)	Brief fame, quick temper, scandal, good for military, sports, law, church, science. Headstrong. Studious. Possible violent death. The stars of the belt are often called the Three Kings.
	Good fortune, success, fame, shrewd, rash, changeable, inventive, determined, a rebel, fevers, acute illness.
Mercury/Venus. Or Venus with Jupiter influence (Ebertin)	

9th	14° 05' Cancer	Sirius. Alpha Canis Majoris. Greater Dog Star, etc.	2° 40'
9th	20° 14' Cancer	Castor. Alpha Geminorum.	2° 20'
9th	23° 13' Cancer	Pollux. Beta Geminorum.	2° 30'
9th	23° 47'	Procyon. Alpha Canis Minoris. Lesser Dog Star &c.	2° 40'
10th	7° 20' Leo	Praesepe. The Beehive Cluster, traditionally The Manger.	1 degree, to avoid Aselli influence.
11th	13° 20' Leo	Kochab. Beta Ursa Minoris.	
11th	13° 39' Leo	Sertan or Accubens. Alpha Cancri.	1° 30'
12th	29° 50' Leo	Alphard. Alpha Hydrae.	2° 20'
12th	29° 50' Leo	Regulus, Alpha Leo. Cor Leonis.	2° 30'
12th	7° 27' Virgo	Thuban. Alpha Draconis. Dragon's Tail.	1° 00'

Jupiter/Mars	Luck, pride, wealth, ambition, good reputation, fame, honours, occult interests, dog bites. Honour and good will, the favour of men and of aerial spirits, gives power to pacify and reconcile kings, princes and other men. Behenian.
Mercury/Jupiter	Good nature, morals, manners. With Sun or Mars energy and satire.
Strong Mars influence	Can be brutal, tyrannical and cruel.
Mercury/Mars	Confers the favour of the gods, spirits and men; protects from evil magics and preserves health. Behenian.
Moon/Mars, Ebertin adds with Neptune influence.	Malefic, bad for eyesight; infectious disease and addiction. Chinese astrology associates it with ancestors and with a lunar conjunction it grants strange experience involving the world of the dead, or mediumship. A necromancer's star, to be handled with care. Flanked closely by the Aselli, must really be taken together.
Saturn/Venus	Little studied.
Mars/Saturn	A sinister star, conducive to deceit and mental instability.
Saturn with a measure of Venus and Neptune (Ebertin).	Unfortunate: poisons, poisonous bites and suffocation, etc.
Mars/Jupiter	A Royal Star: glory, wealth, and great honours, chiefly by military preferment, makes a man temperate, appeases wrath and gives favour. Behenian.
Saturn/Mars	A former Pole Star with much attendant lore.

13th	15° 42' Virgo	Mizar, Tail of the Great Bear.	2° 10'
14th	26° 56' Virgo	Alkaid (Benetnash). Tail of Ursa Major.	2° 20'
15th	0° Libra	Equinoctial point.	
15th	10° 44' Libra	Gienah. Gamma Corvus. Wing of the Crow.	1° 40'
16th	13° 27' Libra	Alkorab/Algorab. Delta Corvus.	1° 40'
16th	23° 50' Libra	Spica. Alpha Virginis.	2° 40'
16th	24° 14' Libra	Arcturus. Alpha Bootis. Alcameth.	2° 40'
17th	28° 06' Libra	Izar. Epsilon Bootis. Pulcherrima, the Loveliest.	2° 00'
18th	11° 51' Scorpio	Acrux. Alpha Crucis. The Southern Cross.	2° 30'
18th	12° 18' Scorpio	Alphecca or Elepheia, Alpha Coronae Borealis.	2° 10'

Mars	Conducive to conflagrations and massacres.
Mars/ Uranus/Saturn (Ebertin). Perhaps Moon/Mercury or Mercury/Mars in traditional terms.	'Availeth against incantations, and maketh a man secure in his travels'. It is worth noting that the full name of this star in Arabic refers to female professional mourners of the type associated with the origins of goetia (see *Geosophia*, etc). It is counted a malefic star. Behenian.
Saturn/Mars (Agrippa)	Courage, 'naughty dreams', can expel evil spirits or gather them together, good against the malice of men, devils, and winds. Behenian.
Saturn/Mars	Strengthens the restraining and limiting nature of Saturn.
Venus/Mercury.	Wealth, fame, honour, victory. Sacred to Ishtar the Virgin. Most benign Fixed Star. Behenian.
Mars when aspected fully by the Sun. Jupiter otherwise.	Success through patient labour. Storms upon the Earth, but riches and honour to those born under it. Behenian.
Mercury/Saturn	Much odd modern speculation, little astrological use currently, but Bootes is an important magical constellation.
Jupiter	Most potent for good on the Ascendant, given a favourable Scorpio. Bestows aptitude and insight in occult or mystical matters. A major Southern hemisphere star.
Venus/Mercury	Behenian.

19th	22° 04' Scorpio	Unukalhai. Alpha Serpentis.	2° 10'
19th	29° 29' Scorpio	Toliman or Bungula, Alpha Centauri.	2° 40'
20th	09° 46' Sagittarius	Antares. Alpha Scorpius, Cor Scorpionis.	2° 30'
20th	11° 58' Sagittarius	Alwaid. Beta Draconis, Rastaban.	1° 40'
20th	16° 09' Sagittarius	Alpha Hercules. Ras Algethi; Head of the kneeling Hercules.	1° 30'
21st	22° 27' Sagittarius	Ras Alhaque. Head of Opiuchus.	2° 10'
22nd	0° Capricorn	Solsticial point.	
22nd	1° 04' Capricorn	Spiculum, the spear.	1° 00'
23rd	15° 19' Capricorn	Vega. Alpha Lyrae. Falling Vulture.	2° 40'
24th	1° 47' Aquarius	Altair. Alpha Aquila.	2° 40'
25th	23° 33' Aquarius	Deneb Algedi. Delta Capricorni. Tail of the Goat.	1° 40'

Saturn/Mars	Suicide, insanity, accidents, chronic disease. Success in war, politics, writing. Problems in love, shipwreck.
Venus/Jupiter	Friends and honour, possible problems relating to women, fatalism.
Mars/Jupiter	A Royal Star: Behenian.
Saturn/Mars	
Mars/Venus with a slight influence from Mercury (Ebertin)	Problems or popularity with women, drive for power, courage, boldness, power, fame.
Saturn, some undesirable Venus influence (Ebertin)	
Moon/Mars (Ptolemy).	One of many Fixed Stars associated with blindness, and of ill omen.
Venus/Mercury	Gives power over devils and beasts. Behenian.
Mars/Jupiter	Success, boldness, courage, possible bloodshed and danger from reptiles.
Saturn/Jupiter	Bestoweth prosperity and increaseth wrath. Behenian.

26th	3° 52' Pisces	Fomalhaut. Alpha Piscis Austrinus.	2° 30'
27th	5° 20' Pisces	Deneb Adige. Alpha Cygni.	2° 30'
	23° 28'	Markab. Alpha Pegasi.	2° 00'
28th	29° 22' Pisces	Scheat. Beta Pegasi. Menkib. Shoulder of the Horse.	2° 00'

Ptolemy gives Mercury/Venus. Ebertin adds 'with a blending of Neptune influence'.	A very famous star, the only one of the Four Royal stars not among the Behenians. It falls very close to the cusp of the next Mansion, which arguably places it there (an argument for unequal Mansions is beyond the scope of this treatise). It is predominantly but not wholly good, depending on aspects, etc.
Mercury/Venus	
Mars/Mercury	Honour, fortune, violence, fevers, death by violence.
Strong Saturn (Ebertin) Mars/Mercury	

In using the Lunar Mansions astrologically, we may, of course, note and employ the planetary positions, particularly conjunctions and aspects with the Moon and various stars. So too, just as in conventional astrology we may legitimately focus on the Moon's position in the solar Zodiac Signs, we would be remiss in failing to note the Sun's motion through the Mansions. The pre-Islamic Bedouin's Anwa calendar, featuring observation of the rising and settings of major fixed stars at Sunrise, involves precisely such a division of the year into 28 parts. Subsequently Anwa merged with Arabic 'Manzil' Mansion lore, as time-related symbol sets with equal numbers of parts are prone to doing. There is thus nothing strange or unusual about applying the Mansions to the solar year. While solar conjunctions with stars are to be avoided, relations between Sun and Moon in calendrics are close. When the Moon is Full, the Sun's position is precisely opposite hers, and from her observable relation to the stars, his precise position, for example in relation to a Solstice point, may be deduced. In essence, the Mansions are a stellar map against which backdrop the planets and luminaries move. Thus, the Mansions may also be used to divide the solar year, with the 1st, 8th, 15th and 22nd Mansions corresponding to the Equinoxes and Solstices. Other significant points may also be observed, as here with Thelemic, Sabbatic, and Egyptian calendrics for examples.

THE MANSIONS AS MAP OF THE SOLAR YEAR

1 – 0 Aries, March 21st. Feast for the Supreme Ritual, Equinox.

2 – 13 Aries April 3rd. 3 days of the writing of AL on 8th, 9th, 10th.

3 – 26 Aries April 16th.

4 – 9 Taurus April 30th Walpurgisnacht.

5 – 21 Taurus May 12th.

6 – 4 Gemini May 26th. Begins 2nd Egyptian month Chenthi/ Horus.

7 – 17 Gemini June 8th.

8 – 0 Cancer June 21st. Solstice.

9 – 13 Cancer July 5th.

10 – 26 Cancer July 19th.

11 – 9 Leo Aug 2nd.

12 – 21 Leo Aug 14th 12th is Feast for the Prophet and his Bride.

13 – 4 Virgo Aug 28th 29th begins Egyptian month Thoth.

14 – 17 Virgo Sept 10th.

15 – 0 Libra Sept 21st Equinox, equals 26th of Thoth, contest of Set and Horus.

16 – 13 Libra Oct 7th.

17 – 26 Libra Oct 20th.

18 – 9 Scorpio Nov 2nd (close to Samhain, All Hallows, etc.).

19 – 21 Scorpio Nov 14th. Equals 17th Hathor, death of Osiris.

20 – 4 Sagittarius Nov 27th. Begins Egyptian month Sechet.

21 – 17 Sagittarius Dec 10th.

22 – 0 Capricorn Dec 21st. Solstice.

23 – 13 Capricorn Jan 4th.

24 – 26 Capricorn Jan 17th.

25 – 9 Aquarius Jan 29th.

26 – 21 Aquarius Feb 10th.

27 – 4 Pisces Feb 23rd 25th. Begins 11th Egyptian month.

28 – 17 Pisces Mar 8th.

APPENDIX

THE LUNAR MANSIONS IN AGRIPPA AND THE *PICATRIX*

Agrippa's chapter on the images of the Lunar Mansions follows. He is partly extracting from an astrological work of Ibn Al-Hatim rather than the *Picatrix*. While his incenses and images broadly agree, Agrippa devotes more space to the purposes or powers of the Mansions, where Al-Hatim usually gives one only per Mansion. What Agrippa removes is the description of the heavens, the name of the Lords of the Mansion, and magical procedures involving them and their names. We can legitimately assume circulation of works that included them or similar materials; pseudo-Albertus denounces them, while Agrippa was not unique in his familiarity with them. Al-Hatim's work is of four chapters, of which the fourth is by far the longest, but other introductory astrological matters of interest are outlined in the preceding. These do have a bearing on how the Mansions operate, and the older worldview in which they do so, so I follow Agrippa's example in extraction, removing mostly the formal religious expressions, etc.

In Chapter One, he places the Sun among the six planets, three above, three below, whose periods he also gives: Saturn ('the Killer'): traverses a Sign in thirty months and the zodiac in 30 years approximately (28 would have been more germane perhaps). Jupiter, a Sign per year, the Zodiac in twelve. Mars: 45 days, Zodiac in eighteen months approximately; Sun, a month and a year respectively. Venus, twenty-five days and ten months respectively. Mercury, eight days and three days twenty-six days, respectively. 'Below it is the Moon; which traverses a zodiacal Sign in two nights, and the sphere (Zodiac) in twenty-eight nights...' 'Lower than the Moon is fire, and lower than fire is air, and lower than air is water, and lower than water is earth' (the sublunary, elemental world).

In his second chapter he speaks of the Signs 'aspecting' one another, by which he means the 'opposition aspect' specifically. This is a feature emphasised in Arabic astrology, and easily followed when forewarned. Thus Aries is opposite – and thus 'aspects' – Libra; Taurus, Scorpio; Gemini, Sagittarius, Cancer, Capricorn; Leo, Aquarius; Virgo, Pisces. In each case the seventh Sign following, and as one rises in the East, the other sets in the West. 'Similarly the Mansions aspect one another' only counting the fourteenth.

The third chapter simply gives titles to the planets typical of their power and asks for God's deliverance from all of them. Late Antiquity would have understood his frame of reference; deliverance from the agents of Fate, i.e. the planetary gods, was a promise of the soteriological Mystery cults. Hermetic magic, deeply astrological and mythological at once, confronted the same problem by other means.

OF THE IMAGES OF THE MANSIONS OF THE MOON.
(TBOP II CHAP. XLVI AND BM BOOK I. II. XLIV)

They made also images for every mansion of the Moon.

In the first for the destruction of someone, they made in an iron ring, the image of a black man in a garment made of hair, and girdled round, casting a small lance with his right hand; they sealed this in black wax, and perfumed it with liquid storax, and wished some evil to come.

In the second, against the wrath of the prince, and for reconciliation with him, they sealed in white wax and mastic, the image of a king crowned, and perfumed it with lignum aloes.

In the third, they made an image in a silver ring, whose table was square, the figure of which was a woman well clothed, sitting in a chair, her right hand being lifted up on her head; they sealed it and perfumed it with musk, camphire and calamus aromaticus. They affirmed that this giveth happy fortune and every good thing.

In the fourth, for revenge, separation, enmity and ill will, they sealed in red wax the Image of a soldier sitting on an horse, holding a serpent in his right hand; they perfumed it with red myrrh, and storax.

In the fifth, for the favour of kings and officers, and good entertainment, they sealed in silver the head of a man, and perfumed it with sanders.

In the sixth, for to procure love betwixt two, they sealed in white wax two images embracing one another, and perfumed them with lignum aloes and amber.

In the seventh, for to obtain every good thing, they sealed in silver the image of a man well clothed, holding up his hands to heaven as it were praying and supplicating, and perfumed it with good odours.

In the eighth, for victory in war, they made a seal of tin, being an image of an eagle having the face of a man, and perfumed it with brimstone.

In the ninth, to cause infirmities, they made a seal of lead, being the image of a man wanting his privy parts, shutting his eyes with his hands; and they perfumed it with rosin of the pine.

In the tenth, to facilitate child-bearing, and to cure the sick, they made a seal of gold, being the head of a lion, and perfumed it with amber.

In the eleventh, for fear, reverence and worship, they made a seal of a plate of gold, being the image of a man riding on a lion, holding the ear thereof in his left hand, and in his right, holding forth a bracelet of gold, and they perfumed it with good odours and saffron.

In the twelfth, for the separation of lovers, they made a seal of black lead, being the image of a dragon fighting with a man, and they perfumed it with the hairs of a lion, and asafetida.

In the thirteenth, for the agreement of married couples, and for the dissolving of charms against copulation, they made a seal of the images of both, of the man in red wax, of the woman in white, and caused them to embrace one another, perfuming it with lignum aloes and amber.

In the fourteenth, for divorce and separation of the man from the woman, they made a seal of red copper, being the image of a dog biting his tail, and they perfumed it with the hair of a black dog, and black cat.

In the fifteenth, for to obtain friendship and good will, they made the image of a man sitting, and inditing [writing, or possibly dictating] of letters, and perfumed it with frankincense and nutmegs.

In the sixteenth, for to gain much merchandising they made a seal of silver, being the image of a man sitting upon a chair, holding a balance in his hand, and they perfumed it with well smelling spices.

In the seventeenth, against thieves and robbers, they sealed with an iron seal the image of an ape, and perfumed it with the hair of an ape.

In the eighteenth, against fevers and pains of the belly, they made a seal of copper, being the image of a snake holding his tail above his head, and they perfumed it with hartshorn, and reported the same seal to put to flight serpents, and all venomous creatures from the place where it is buried.

In the nineteenth for facilitating birth, and provoking the menstrues, they made a seal of copper, being the image of a woman holding her hands upon her face; and they perfumed it with liquid storax.

In the twentieth, for hunting, they made a seal of tin, being the image of *Sagittary* [Sagittarius], half a man and half an horse, and they perfumed it with the head of a wolf.

In the twenty-one for the destruction of somebody, they made the image of a man with a double countenance, before and behind, and they perfumed it with brimstone and jet, and did put it in a box of brass, and with it brimstone and jet, and the hair of him whom they would hurt.

In the two and twentieth, for the security of runaways, they made a seal of iron, being the image of a man with wings on his feet, bearing an helmet on his head, and they perfumed it with argent vive.

In the three and twentieth, for destruction and wasting, they made a seal of iron, being the image of a cat, having a dog's head, and they perfumed it with the hairs of a dog's head, and buried it in the place where they did pretend to hurt.

In the four and twentieth, for the multiplying of herds of cattle, they took the horn of a ram, bull, or goat, or of that sort of cattle which they would increase, and sealed in it burning with an iron seal, the image of a woman giving suck [breast feeding] to her son, and they hanged it on the neck of that cattle who was the leader of the flock, or they sealed it in his horn.

In the five and twentieth, for the preservation of trees and harvests, they sealed in the wood of a figure [Barrett has 'fig-tree', which is more likely correct], the image of a man planting, and they perfumed it with the flowers of the fig-tree, and did hang it on the tree.

In the six and twentieth for love and favour, they sealed

in white wax and mastic the image of a woman washing and combing her hairs, and they perfumed it with things smelling very well.

In the seven and twentieth for to destroy fountains, pits, medicinal waters and baths, they made of red earth the image of a man winged, holding in his hand an empty vessel, and perforated, and the image being burnt, they did put in the vessel asafetida, and liquid storax, and they did overwhelm and bury it in the pond or fountain which they would destroy.

In the eight and twentieth, for to gather fishes together, they made a seal of copper, being the image of a fish, and they perfumed it with the skin of a sea fish, and did cast it into the water, wheresoever they would have the fish to gather together.

Moreover together with the foresaid Images, they did write down also the names of the spirits and their characters, and did invocate and pray for those things which they pretended to obtain.[20] (My emphasis – 'Sagittary' identifies match of sign and constellation when composed. Note necessity of sigils and characters plus ritual procedure.)

---

20 Heinrich Cornelius Agrippa, *Three Books of Occult Philosophy*, trans. by James Freake, ed. by Donald Tyson (St. Paul: Llewellyn, 1993) pp 392-93.

TALISMANS AND WORKS OF THE LUNAR MANSIONS FROM THE
PICATRIX

Translation by Soror Scorpio and Frater Althotash

One needs to know the constellation which is
sympathetic to the talismanic rite intended.
Therefore in this chapter I set forth the nature of
the works performed under the lunar mansions.
The maker of talismans must know the ephemeris,
as also the constellations and be sure lest his works
come to naught.

The Reasonable Soul is applied by Will to the
World Soul and is in accord with it. By this do
our works come to pass. In knowledge of the stars
and planets is the beginning of that application
and of the Art of Talismans. In these operations
following one needs to know the position of the
Moon and in which of Her Mansions She is
situated; and thus it is I recount the nature of those
Mansions according to the Indians, that knowing
Her position, and Her potency therein you might
work aright the Art of Talismans.

1. The first station of Mansion is called Al Saratan, of the
beginning of Aries unto 12 degrees 51' 26" of Aries. In
this Mansion one may make journeys, it is also good for
purgatives. Talismans for journeys in safety; for marriage
matches and friendships when these are needed, either
to make or to mend. Also to regain a runaway slave or

to assist him, or to destroy associations. In operations of good take note of the evil planets and be free of them, also the combustion of the Sun. In operations of the bad, combustion may however be desirable.

2. Al Butan. 12 degrees 51' 26" of Aries until 25° 42' 52" of the Ram. Good for the digging of canals, fountains and the like; also to request objectives and to bury treasure or take from it. Talismans for the good of seed crops, further for the escape of slaves and the arrest of prisoners and the putting to torture.

3. Al Turaija. 25° 42' 52" Aries unto 8° 34' 18" of Taurus. Talismans for the distressed in need of liberation. Also to destroy companionship and to free or to enchain captives. Further for the success in alchemical operations, for hunting, love in marriage, injury of herds and slaves to the destruction of their lords.

4). Al Dabarah. 8° 34' 18" to 21° 25' 44" of Taurus. Talismans to damage a tower or contrariwise ensure duration of buildings. Also to crops and slaves, their destruction or maintenance. Also to cause estrangement of married partners. Also for diggings, for water or treasure and buried things, it causes hostility, and to banish evil vermin, as serpents and snakes.

5. Al Haq'a. 21° 25' 44" to 4° 17' 10" of Gemini. To teach and to instruct and to thrive in instruction, in religion, clerical and manual learning. To preserve travellers and enterprises. To preserve buildings and destroy company. To bring unity and harmony in marriage when the Moon and the Ascendant are in a Human Sign under good

aspect. The Human Signs are the Twins, the Virgin, Libra, the Archer and the Waterbearer.

6. Al Han'ah. 4° 17' 10" to 17° 18' 36" to annihilate towns and to prosecute. To chastise kings. To cover enemies with evil. To destroy crops and store of goods. Also for good relationships, good hunting, also to hinder the normal efficacy of medicine.

7. Al Dira. 17° 18' 36" to the end of Gemini. For thriving trade, growth of crops, safety of relationships among friends. To bind vermin, as flies and such, to keep them from a place. Alchemy under this station will fail and need repeating. A talisman for demands of great men and their affection. For the flight of slaves, to gut houses and remove store of goods and possessions.

8. Al Natra. 0° Cancer til 12° 51' 26". Talismans of love and friendship where there is none. Preserving travellers and friendships. Also to retain prisoners and cause slaves to be wicked. Further to cause the banishing of mice and bugs.

9. Al Tarfas. 12° 51' 26" to 25° 42' 52" Cancer. To destroy crops and land and travellers. To destroy companionships and damage legal proceedings.

10. Al Gabha. 25° 42' 52" Cancer till 8° 34' 18" Leo. Talismans of preserving marriage, to amaze and perplex enemies, to fetter prisoners, to procure durability of buildings and provide harmony with others for mutual profit.

11. Al Zubra. 8° 34' 18" unto 21° 28' 44" Leo. Therein one makes talismans to release prisoners and captives, to the siege of towns, for prosperity of trade, the welfare of travels, the durability of building works and of relations between companions.

12. Al Sarfa. 21° 25' 44" Leo till 4° 17' 10" Virgo. Therein one makes talismans for prosperity of crops and plants, to the destruction of the property of a people. Further talismans to destroy ships or to succeed in alchemy, to keep slaves in right condition.

13. Al Aiwa. 4° 17' 10" to 17° 8' 36" Virgo. Therein one makes talismans that trade might prosper and crops likewise. For the welfare of travellers, to bring about marriage, to free prisoners, to bring union with kings and great men.

14. Al Simak. 17° 8' 36" till full 30 degrees Virgo. Talismans to preserve good relationships between married couples and health through medical treatment. Also talismans to damage seeds, crops and plants and the annihilation of money deposits to cause evil to happen to travellers. For the well-being of kings and luck in navigation and understanding between companions.

15. Al Gafr. 0° to 12° 51' 26" Libra. Talismans for digging of wells and to take possession of buried treasure. To hinder travellers, to separate married couples and destroy good relationships with hostility. To expel enemies and remove them from positions as well as to destroy lodgings and houses.

16. Al Zabana. 12° 51' 26" to 25° 42' 52" Libra. Talismans to damage trade business and crops, either grown or sown. To separate friends and couples. Further if you wish to punish a woman, your wife. Talismans to cause discord amongst friends on journeys, talismans to create discord between companions and to free prisoners.

17. Al Ilkil. 25° 42' 52" Libra to 8° 34' 18" Scorpio. Talismans for wellbeing and good condition of domestic beasts. For the siege of towns and security of buildings. Good journeys by sea. To restore friendships. Particularly good for friendship.

18. AL Qalb. 8° 34' 18" to 21° 25' 44" Scorpio. Talismans to raise the flags of conquering kings over lands of your enemies. Talismans for the solid condition of buildings. Whoever would take a wife while Mars is in this Station will leave her soon a widow, and had best avoid this Mansion. Talismans for the escaping of slaves, for prosperity of plants and secure journeys of sailors, and to the discord of companions.

19. Al Saula. 21° 25' 44" Scorpio to 4° 17' 10" Sagittarius. Talismans for sieges and the defeating of enemies and to take from them what one will. To destroy the prosperity of a people, to separate persons and create discord. Talismans for the well-being of travellers, thriving of crops, flight and escape of slaves from their masters, the sinking of ships and causing shipwrecks, discord of companions, escaping of prisoners and captives.

20. Al Na-a-im. 4° 17' 10" to 17° 8' 36" Sagittarius. Talismans to tame great and difficult beasts. For the quick course and abbreviation of journeys, to bring a person to you, for friendship. Otherwise to aggravate losses of captives and to bring good relationships of a company to ruin.

21. Al Baldah. 17° 8' 36" unto 30 degrees Sagittarius. Talismans for durability of building works, thriving of seeds, further talismans for beasts of burden and transport, as for cattle. To preserve a lords property, safe journeys, to release and keep a woman from her spouse.

22. Al Sa'd Al Dabih. 0° to 12° 51' 26" Capricorn. Talismans to assist the treatment of disease. Talismans to separate couples, to bring about the adultery of a married woman one desires. For the escape of slaves and their flight from the country.

23. Al Sa'd Bula. 12° 51' 26" to 25° 42' 52" Capricorn. Therein one makes Talismans for the treatment of disease, talismans for the annihilation of property, for the separation of couples and the liberation or discharge of captives.

24. Al Sa'd Al Su-ud. 25° 42' 52" Capricorn to 8° 34' 18" Aquarius. Therein one makes talismans for the flourishing of business and the unity of married couples. Talismans for the victory of armies and troops. On the other hand for the discord of companions and the freeing of captives. Alchemical operations under this sign will fail.

25. Al Sa'd Al Ahbija. 8° 34' 18" to 21° 25' 44" Aquarius. Talismans for the siege of towns. Talismans to the injury of enemies and victory over them, and division and hostility among them. Talismans for the consignment of messages and spies and to ensure their success. Talismans to separate married couples, destruction of plants and operations of ligature both of the genitalia and of the other members, also to bind captives (it is easy to bind captives in this station). Talismans for the foundation of building works, ensuring safety and durability.

26. Al Farq Al Mugaddam. 21° 25' 44" Aquarius to 4° 17' 10" Pisces. Herein one makes all sorts of talismans for good purposes, and for the binding of souls in love, or whatever a traveller wishes he will obtain, talismans for successful sea journeys, for discord of companions and for binding and fettering of prisoners.

27. Al Farq Al Mu-ahhr. 4° 17' 10" to 17° 8' 36" Pisces. Talismans ensuring the flourishing of trade and a blessed yield of crops. Quick recovery from disease, changes wealth to ruin, sows discord between couples, to prolong the captivity of prisoners and corrupt slaves.

28. Al Risa. 17° 8' 36" to 30° Pisces. Therein one composes talismans for the flourishing of trade and growth of crops, healing diseases, that money be lost, safe journeys, reconciliation of couples, further talismans to bind captives and prevent damage to journeying ships.

AFTERWORD: SOMETHING TO PONDER

I want to see if I can clarify something that I take for granted and consider simple, but which seems to be a tad unfamiliar in the wider community.

For some time, I have worked almost exclusively with one grimoire – with a few frills of my own devising, yet everything revolves around that one text.

The *dramatis personae*, as opposed to names dropped in the incantations, are a particular set of 'demons' of varying rank. There are, to clarify, no thwarting angels, least of all on a one-to-one basis. Brief references to the Christian Trinity on occasion are far less substantial a presence than invocations of God and his angels in other texts, almost a token gesture, and not so difficult to sidestep.

This cast includes some who are not all exactly cuddly; to be honest, some of them can be terrifying. That doesn't change the fact I work with them, and frame things in reference to them. All the time.

With me so far? Possibly not if you aren't in the habit of working within the confines of a specific system *and nothing else*; i.e., finding flexibility and scope within a single system rather than regularly gadding off somewhere else. However, unusual though that may be, the real crunch is the next bit.

It's a well-worn trope that the Early Church identified pagan gods with demons. Meanwhile I have a virtual pantheon of spirits who subjectively at least, frame my magical reality. Particularly in the case of the major ones, I consider them worthy of respect and honour, or to put it another way 'worship', or to offer 'cult honours' to.

Essentially, they are my gods; although of course my role as a magician is more active than that of a religious person. They are not just 'my gods' either, subjectively speaking they are THE gods. Were communication simpler, I might – as done in the past – compare mine with those of others, but that's a step too far for the present. Nevertheless, my relations with them do amount to that, and I eventually saw that was the case.

The presence of scraps of theology from elsewhere within *their* rites doesn't change the fact that they fulfil the same role, on much the same basis, as the deities of an archaic local cult. It certainly helps to know how a 'cult' of this kind worked in the past, which helped the penny drop with me eventually!

However, the difficulties of reviving an ancient cult, even if surmountable, would leave us adrift in many ways. We'd have a few major deities to honour, but the folkloric elements, the lesser members of the cast, and how it all fitted together for magical purposes remains distant in the here and now. Whereas for me, the cast, the rituals and all else is more or less intact, and capable of extension as required.

Do I consider myself a 'diabolist'? No, although as said the early Church deemed all pagan gods demons. A modern pagan with modern gods is a much more appropriate way of looking at what I do.

SELECT BIBLIOGRAPHY

Saint Cyprian (attrib), *Heptameron o Elementos Magicos*, (Venice, 1722) [alleged; the 1810 date is also not to be trusted]

Agrippa, Heinrich Cornelius, *Three Books of Occult Philosophy*, trans. by James Freake, ed. by Donald Tyson (St. Paul: Llewellyn, 1993)

Albertus Magnus *Le Grand Albert*, various editions.

Albertus Magnus, *Speculum Astronomiae* (Approx. 1260)

Albertus Magnus *The Book of the Secrets of Albertus Magnus*, various editions

Albertus Magnus (attrib). *Le Petit Albert*, various editions

Allen, Richard Hinckley, *Star Names and Their Meanings* (New York: G. E. Stechert, 1899)

Barrett, Francis, *The Magus, or Celestial Intelligencer* (London: Lackington, Allen, & Co., 1801)

Betz, Hans Dieter, ed., *The Greek Magical Papyri in Translation* (University of Chicago Press, 1986, 1992)

Betz, Hans Dieter, 'Fragments from a Catabasis Ritual in a Greek Magical Papyrus', *History of Religions*, 19.4 (1980), 287-295

Brady, Bernadette, *Brady's Book of Fixed Stars* (York, Maine: Weiser 1998)

Fontenelle, Julia, Jean Sebastian Eugène, M. Comte, *Nouveau manuel complet des sorciers ou la magie blanche* (Paris: Roret, 1837)

Crowley, Aleister, *The Complete Astrological Writings* (London: Duckworth & Co., 1974)

Crowley, Aleister, *Gems from the Equinox* (Woodbury: Llewellyn, 1974)

de Bergerac, Cyrano, *The Other World: The Comical History of the States and Empires of the Worlds of the Moon and Sun*, trans. by Lovell, A.

(London: Henry Rhodes, 1687)

Ebertin, Reinhold and George Hoffman, *Fixed Stars and Their Interpretation* (Washington: American Federation of Astrologers, 1971)

Ebertin, Reinhold and George Hoffman, *The Combination of Stellar Influences* (Washington: American Federation of Astrologers, 1972)

Huson, Paul, *Mastering Witchcraft* (New York: G.P. Putnam's, 1970)

Huson, Paul, *The Devil's Picturebook*, (London: Abacus, 1971)

Levi, Eliphas, *Dogme et Rituel de la Haute Magie* (Paris: C. Baillere, 1861)

Levi, Eliphas, *Magical Ritual of the Sanctum Regnum Interpreted by the Tarot Trumps*, trans. by William Wynn Westcott (London: George Redway, 1896)

Luck, Georg, *Arcana Mundi: Magic and the Occult in the Greek and Roman Worlds* (New York: Johns Hopkins University Press, 1985)

Mead, G. R. S., ed., *Thrice-Greatest Hermes*, Volume 2 (London: The Theosophical Publishing Society, 1906)

Moulth, Nathaniel. *Petit Manuel du Devin et du Sorcier* (Paris: Passard, 1854)

Nagel, Alexandra, *Marriage with Elementals From Le Comte de Gabalis to a Golden Dawn Ritual* (Master of Arts thesis, University of Amsterdam, 2007)

Paracelsus (Theophrastus von Hohenheim), *Four Treatises by Theophrastus von Hohenheim Called Paracelsus*, ed. by Henry E. Sigerist (Baltimore: Johns Hopkins Press, 1941)

Pausanias, *The Description of Greece*, Volume III, trans. by Thomas Taylor (London: Priestley and Weale, 1824)

Plaisance, Christopher A., *Evocating the Gods: divine evocation in the Greco-Egyptian Magical Papyri* (London: Avalonia Books, 2019)

Pope, Alexander, *The Rape of the Lock* (London: Smithers, 1896)

Robson. Vivian E., *The Fixed Stars and Constellations* (London: Cecil Palmer, 1923)

Scot, Reginald, *Discoverie of Witchcraft*, (London: Stock, 1886)

Scott, Walter, *Letters on Witchcraft and Demonology* (London: Routledge and Sons, 1887)

Shakespeare, William, 'A Midsummer Night's Dream', in *The Globe Illustrated Shakespeare*, ed. by Howard Staunton (New York: Greenwich House, 1986)

Stratton-Kent, Jake, *Geosophia: The Argo of Magic* (London: Scarlet Imprint, 2010)

Stratton-Kent, Jake, *Frimost & Klepoth* (West Yorkshire: Hadean Press, 2011)

Stratton-Kent, Jake, *Pandemonium: A Discordant Concordance of Diverse Spirit Catalogues* (West Yorkshire: Hadean Press, 2016)

Stratton-Kent, Jake, *The Testament of Cyprian the Mage* (London: Scarlet Imprint, 2014)

Stratton-Kent, Jake, *The True Grimoire* (London: Scarlet Imprint, 2009)

Stratton-Kent, Jake, *The Sworn and Secret Grimoire*, (West Yorkshire: Hadean Press, 2021)

Stratton-Kent, Jake, *Pandemonium: A Discordant Concordance of Diverse Spirit Catalogues* (West Yorkshire: Hadean Press, 2016)

Volney, Constantin-François, *The Ruins: or a Survery of the Revolutions of Empires* (J. Johnson, 1789)

Waite, A. E., *The Occult Sciences: A Compendium of Transcendental Doctrine and Experiment* (London: Kegan Paul, 1891)

Weinstock, Stefan, 'Lunar Mansions and Early Calendars', *The Journal of Hellenic Studies*, 69 (1949)

INDEX OF TABLES

General Index

A

Agrippa von Nettesheim, Heinrich Cornelius 9, 10, 13, 15, 24-25, 26,
    35-36, 90, 92, 109-110, 124, 125, 126, 127, 128, 129
Ahrimanes 82, 127
Air 72, 96, 97, 108
    Fomalhaut 68
    spirits of 5
Alphabet of the Magi 55, 90
angels 9, 59, 108–111, 113,
animal symbols 35, 42, 91
    see also Lunar animals.
Arabic Parts 14
Arcana Mundi 31
Aries Equinoctial point 24
Ascendant 27, 136
astrological charts 15–16, 17-20, 27–28
    combustion 28
    Electional 15, 28

B

Baalberith 68, 70
Beelzébuth 70
Behenian stars 26, 81, 92, 124
Betz, Hans Dieter 29, 30

C

Cardinal Signs 24, 72
Cazimi 15
Cerberus 31
chiefs of spirits 67–68
    Four Chiefs 5, 70
Chinese mansion system 34, 39. 40, 68, 105
    astrology 126, 135
Codex Cromwellianus 39

O

Olympians 97
Ormuzd 123
Orpheus 29, 31

P

Palingene 110–113, 115
Pandemonium 73, 163
Paracelsus 82, 84, 110
Paralda 49, 55, 62, 68, 74, 86–89, 90–91, 96
    as Queen of the Sylphs 70, 82–83
Part of Fortune 14–15, 16
Path of the Moon 26
Persephone 6, 9, 83, 97
Petit Manuel du Devin et du Sorcier 49
Picatrix 25, 92, 98
planetary aspects 15, 57, 142
    plotting 19–20
Prayer of the Salamanders 54, 82, 89
Precession of the Equinoxes 26
Pressine 102, 117
Ptolemy 13, 19–20
Puck 122
Pyramidos 97

R

Renaissance Astrology 13–16, 28

S

Saint Cyprian 48, 73, 99, 120
Salamander 65
Saturday 6, 40, 56, 96
Saturn 5, 40, 56, 87
    see also Seal of Saturn.
Scot, Reginald 83, 116, 120, 121, 122
Scott, Sir Walter 65, 69, 108, 110, 119–122
Seal of Jupiter 60

www.ingramcontent.com/pod-product-compliance
Lightning Source LLC
Chambersburg PA
CBHW072230270326
41930CB00010B/2074